Tools

German – English
English – German

by Stefan Riedel

From my Technical Dictionary Series

Bibliographic information by the German National Library:

The German National Library (Deutsche Nationalbibliothek) lists this publication in the German National Bibliography (Deutsche Nationalbibliografie); detailed bibliographic data are available on the Internet at http://www.d-nb.de.

Author: Stefan Riedel, » Tools «
Internet: www.riedel-author.com
E-mail: info@riedel-autor.de

First edition
© 2026 Stefan Riedel
All rights reserved.

Editorial support: Anke Lietmann, Marl, Germany
Setting: Satz+Layout Werkstatt Kluth GmbH, Erftstadt, Germany
Book cover: UlinneDesign, Neuenkirchen, Germany
          Ulrike Linnenbrink
Publisher: BoD · Books on Demand GmbH, Überseering 33,
22297 Hamburg, bod@bod.de
Print: Libri Plureos GmbH, Friedensallee 273, 22763 Hamburg

ISBN: 978-3-7583-2924-1

Preface

This technical dictionary is ideal for craftsmen who regularly need German technical terms for their work. Whether you order something from abroad, write offers or maybe just want to be able to talk to your international co-workers on the construction-site: just like a toolbox, this dictionary holds the vocabulary necessary for successful technical communication in German. Unified communication has become extremely important in today's business world in order to successfully complete building projects together with co-workers from other countries.

This technical dictionary ,Tools' offers you a comprehensive collection of technical terms translated from German to English and vice versa with a clear, reader-friendly layout which helps you to find the right word quickly and easily.

One special feature of this technical dictionary is your personalized section at the end of the book. You can add ,Your personal 100 words of everyday life' (general terms) and ,Your personal 100 words from professional practice' (technical terms). This practical section is your personal catalogue in which you can find the most frequently used words for your daily needs, adapted to your technical communication in German.

It is very important to me to offer you a dictionary in which you can find German technical terms quickly and easily and use them for a wide range of everyday situations.

My principle is: ,Words travel around the world and connect people'.

Words form sentences; the sentences form texts and are the foundation of communication.

Whether spoken or written.

Increase your German vocabulary with this technical dictionary, improve your technical German and make your language skills the basis for an international career in a global economy. Today, global communication is not only necessary but an essential prerequisite for everyday life, education, studies, professional life, etc.

If you have any positive or negative criticism or suggestions concerning this series of technical dictionaries, please feel free to contact me. I am grateful for your feedback.

List of abbreviations

BE   British English
       The word is used primarily or solely in British English.

AE   American English
       The word is used primarily or solely in American English.

ugs.   umgangssprachlich
       colloquial expression; not technical terminology (German words)

coll.   colloquial
       colloquial expression; not technical terminology (English words)

f   female grammatical gender, feminine noun (die)
m   male grammatical gender, male noun (der)
n   neuter grammatical gender, neuter noun (das)

pl   Plural
       The word is used primarily or solely in the plural form.

sg   Singular
       The word is used primarily or solely in the singular form.

®   registered trademark (rightholder indicated in parentheses)

Further abbreviations used in this book:

e.g.   exempli gratia/for example
etc.   et cetera/and so forth
fin.   financial
pol.   political
z. B.   zum Beispiel/for example

Translations

- with different meanings are indicated by consecutive numbering for better clarity.
- with same or similar meaning are not indicated by consecutive numbering.
- with same or similar meaning within a number are separated by a slash.

Explanations:

Additional information in parentheses serves to spec fy the term or assign it to a special subject area.

In order to improve the readability and findab lity, we have refrained from adding abbreviations for the technical subject areas. The special field of the technical terms contained in this book can be found in the summary.

German – English

A

Abbeizer *m*	paint remover
	paint stripper
Abbeizmittel *n*	paint remover
	paint stripper
Abbrechklinge *f*	snap-off blade
Abdeckband *n*	masking tape
Abdeckfolie *f*	cover sheeting
Abend *m*	evening
Abfluss *m*	drain
Abisoliermesser *n*	cable stripping knife
Abisolierzange *f*	wire stripper
Abklebeband *n*	masking tape
ablegen	discard, to
Abmessung *f*	dimension
Abrichtblock *m* (Siliziumkarbid)	flattening stone
Abrichtblock *m* (Stahl)	lapping plate
Absetzmulde *f*	skip
Absetzsäge *f*	crosscut saw
Absetzsägeblatt *n*	cross-cut blade
Absperrventil *n*	shut-off valve
Abstechstahl Diamantform *m*	diamond parting tool
Abstechstahl *m*	parting tool
Abstechstahl Messerform *m*	knife shaped parting tool
abziehen	hone, to
Abziehöl *n*	honing-oil
Abziehpaste *f*	honing compound
Abziehstein *m*	honing stone
Aceton *nsg*	acetone *sg*
Achillesferse *f (ugs.)*	Achilles' heel *(coll.)*
	weak spot *(coll.)*

Achteck *n*	octagon
Achtung *fsg*	attention *sg*
Acryl *nsg*	acrylic *sg*
Acrylfarbe *f*	acryl paint
Adresse *f*	address
Ahle *f*	awl
	stabbing awl
ähnlich	similar
Akkuschrauber *m*	cordless screwdriver
Alarm *m*	alarm
Alarmanlage *f*	alarm system
Alkohol *m*	alcohol
Alkoholverbot *n*	ban on alcohol
allen Widrigkeiten zum Trotz	against all odds
alt	old
Altöl *n*	used oil (e.g. drained from the engine of a vehicle)
Aluminium *nsg*	aluminium *sg (BE)*
	aluminum *sg (AE)*
Amboss *m*	anvil
anders	different
Anfahrtsbeschreibung *f*	directions *pl*
angegeben	specified
Angestellter *m*	white-collar worker *(coll.)*
anheben (Last)	lift, to
Anleitung *f*	instruction
Anreißmesser *n*	marking knife
Anreißnadel *f*	scriber
	stabbing awl
Anreißschablone *f*	saddle square
Anschlag *m* (Stahlmaßstab)	ruler stop
anschlagen	sling, to

Anschlagmittel *n*	sling gear
	lifting means *pl*
Anschlagpunkt *m*	sling point
	anchor point
Anschrift *f*	address
Anstrichfarbe *f*	paint
April *m*	April
Arbeiter *m*	blue-collar worker *(coll.)*
Arbeitsbühne *f*	work platform
Arbeitskollege *m*	colleague
Arbeitsscheinwerfer *m*	work light
Arbeitsstätte *f*	workplace
Arbeitsstättenverordnung/	Workplaces Ordinance/
ArbStättV *f*	ArbStättV
Arbeitstag *m* (in UK/USA keine	business day
Unterscheidung zum Werktag)	working day
Arbeitsunfall *m*	accident at work
	work accident
Arbeitszeit *f*	working time
Architekt *m*	architect
Argon *nsg*	argon *sg*
Art *f*	type
Asbest *m*	asbestos
Atemschutzmaske *f*	respirator mask
ätzend	corrosive
Ätznatron *nsg*	caustic soda *sg*
auf tönernen Füßen stehen *(ugs.)*	built on sand, to be *(coll.)*
aufregend	exciting
aufschieben	delay, to
aufteilen	split, to
Auftraggeber *m*	client
Aufzug *m*	elevator *(AE)* (lift)
	lift *(BE)*

August *m*	August
Ausbesserungsarbeit *f*	repair work
ausborgen	lend, to
Ausdrehstahl *m* (Holzbearbeitung)	side cutting scraper
Ausdrehstahl rund *m* (Holzbearbeitung)	side cutting scraper round
Ausdrehstahl trapezoid *m* (Holzbearbeitung)	side cutting scraper diamond
ausgelaufen (Flüssigkeit)	leaked out
ausgezeichnet	excellent
Aushöhleisen *n*	hollowing tool
ausleihen	lend, to
ausrangieren	discard, to
ausscheiden	discard, to
Außen-Torx-Schraube *f* (® acument)	external Torx screw (® acument)
Außeneckenkelle *f*	outer corner trowel
Außentaster *m*	outside caliper
außergewöhnlich	extraordinary
aussondern	discard, to
aussuchen	choose, to
auswählen	choose, to select, to
Autokühler *m*	radiator
Automatikkörner *m*	automatic center punch *(AE)* automatic centre punch *(BE)*
automatischer Schweißer-schutzfilter *m*	automatic darkening filter/ADF
Avis *m/n*	advice
Axt *f*	ax *(AE)* axe *(BE)*
Axtstiel *m*	ax handle *(AE)* axe handle *(BE)*
Azeton *nsg*	acetone *sg*

B

Backe *f*	jaw
Bandmaß *n*	measuring tape
	tape measure
Bandschleifer *m*	belt sander
Bankfeiertag *m*	bank holiday *(BE)*
Barettfeile *f*	barrette file
bastard (grob)	bastard (coarse)
	cut 1 (coarse)
Bauchzange *f*	crucible tongs *pl*
Bauholz *n*	lumber
Baujahr *n*	year of construction
Bedienungsanleitung *f*	user guide
	user manual
Bedingung *f*	condition
bei der Arbeit	on the job
beidseitig	double-faced
Beil *n*	hatchet
Beitel *m*	chisel
Beize *f*	wood stain
Belgischer Brocken *m*	Belgian whetstone
Benzin *n*	gas *(AE)*
	gasoline *(AE)*
	petrol *(BE)*
beraten	advise, to
berechnen (fin.)	charge, to
bereitstellen	available, to make
Berliner Maurerhammer *m*	mason's hammer, Berlin type
beschäftigt	busy
bescheiden	modest
Beschwerde *f*	complaint
Besen *m*	broom

B

besonders	especially
	specially
Beton *m*	concrete
Betonbohrer *m*	concrete drill
Betonfertigteil *n*	precast concrete element
Betonmischer *m*	cement mixer
	concrete mixer
Betonschieber *m*	concrete spreader
Betonverteiler *m*	concrete spreader
Betonzange *f*	concrete pliers *pl*
	concretor's pliers *pl*
	mechanic's nippers *pl*
	monier pliers *pl*
	Rabitz pliers *pl*
Betriebsanweisung *f*	operating instructions *pl*
Betriebsgelände *n*	company premises *pl*
	premises *pl*
Betriebssicherheitsverordnung/ BetrSichV *f*	Ordinance on Industrial Safety and Health/BetrSichV
Bienenwachs *n*	beeswax
Bitumen *n*	bitumen
Blech *n*	sheet metal
Blechschere *f*	tin snips *pl*
Blechschraube *f*	sheet metal screw
	tapping screw
Blei *nsg*	lead *sg*
Bleihammer *m*	lead hammer
Bleimesser *n*	lead knife
Blindflansch *m*	blind flange
	blank flange
Blockhaus-Hohlbeitel *m*	framing gauge
Blockhausbeitel *m*	timber frame chisel
Blockhobel *m*	block plane

German	English
Boden *m*	floor
Bodenlegerkelle *f*	flooring trowel
Bodenventil *n*	bottom valve
Bogen *m*	arc
Bogensäge *f*	bow saw
Bohle *f*	plank
Bohrer *m* (für Bohrmaschine)	drill bit
Bohrfutter *n*	drill chuck
Bohrfutterschlüssel *m*	chuck key
Bohrhammer *m*	rotary hammer
Bohrsäge *f*	keyhole saw
Bolzenschneider *m*	bolt cropper bolt cutter
borgen	borrow, to
Brandschutzzeichen *n*	fire protection sign
Brecheisen *n*	crowbar pry bar wrecking bar
Brechstange *f*	crowbar pry bar wrecking bar
breit	wide
Breite *f*	width
Bügelmessschraube *f*	outside micrometer *(AE)* outside micrometre *(BE)*
Bügelsäge *f*	hacksaw
Bundschlitzsäge für Gitarren *f*	fret wire saw guitar saw
Bunsenbrenner *m*	Bunsen burner
Bürste *f*	brush

B

C

C

C-Zwinge *f*	C-clamp
	G-clamp
CE-Kennzeichnung *f*	CE mark
	CE marking
Celsius *n*	Celsius
Chemikalie *f*	chemical
Chrom *nsg*	chrome *sg*
Crimpzange *f*	crimping pliers *pl*
	crimping tool
Cuttermesser *n*	box cutter

D

Dach *n*	roof
Dachdeckerhammer *m*	roofer's hammer
Dachpfanne *f*	pan tile
	roof tile
Dachsbeil *n*	adz *(AE)*
	adze *(BE)*
Dachschindel *f*	roof shingle
Dachtraufe *f*	eaves *pl*
Dachverkleidung *f*	roof panel
Dachziegel *m*	pan tile
	roof tile
Dampf *m*	vapor *(AE)*
	vapour *(BE)*
Dampfdruck *m*	vapor pressure *(AE)*
	vapour pressure *(BE)*
dankbar	grateful
Datum *n*	date
Dechsel *f*	adz *(AE)*
	adze *(BE)*
Dehnungsfugenkelle *f*	cement groover

Dekupiersäge *f*	coping saw
Detail *n*	detail
Deutsche Industrienorm/DIN *f*	German Industrial Standard/DIN
Dezember *m*	December
Diagonalschnitt *m*	diagonal cut
Diamantschleifer *m*	diamond sharpener
Diamantschleifplatte *f*	diamond sharpening plate
Diamantschleifstein *m*	diamond sharpening stone
Dichtungsring *m*	sealing washer
dick (Gegenstand)	thick
Dickenmessgerät *n*	thickness caliper
Dienstag *m*	Tuesday
diese Woche	this week
diesen Monat	this month
dieses Jahr	this year
Dietrich *m*	picklock
Dispersionsfarbe *f*	emulsion paint
Donnerstag *m*	Thursday
Doppel-Gehrungswinkel *m*	miter marking saddle *(AE)* mitre marking saddle *(BE)*
Doppelhobel *m*	jack plane
Doppeltür *f*	double doors *pl*
Draht *m*	wire
Drahtbürste *f*	wire brush
Drechselbank *f*	lathe
Drechselschaber *m*	square end scraper
Dreck *msg*	dirt *sg*
dreckig	dirty
Drehkreuz *n*	lug wrench *(AE)* wheel brace *(BE)* wheel wrench *(BE)*

D

Drehmaschine *f*	lathe
Drehmoment *n*	torque
Drehmomentschlüssel *m*	torque spanner *(BE)* torque wrench *(AE)*
Drehröhre *f*	spindle gouge
Drehröhre, englische Form *f*	spindle gouge, English pattern
Drehröhre, kontinentale Form *f*	spindle gouge, European continental pattern
Dreikant *m/n*	three-square
Dreikantfeile *f*	three-square file triangular file
Drillbohrer *m*	Archimedean drill drill push drill
dringend	urgent
Druck *m*	pressure
druckempfindlich	pressure-sensitive
Druckluft *fsg*	compressed air *sg*
Dübel *m*	screw anchor *(AE)* wall plug *(BE)*
dünn (Gegenstand)	thin
durchgehender Riss *m*	through-crack
Durchmesser *m*	diameter
Dusche *f*	shower

E

Eckenausstecheisen *n*	corner cutting chisel
Eckenhobel *m*	plasterer's plane
Eckenpinsel *m*	corner brush
Eckrohrzange *f*	corner pipe wrench
Edelgas *n*	noble gas
Edelstahl *m*	stainless steel

effektiv	effective
Effektivität *fsg*	effectiveness
effizient	efficient
Effizienz *f*	efficiency
ehrlich	honest
eigenartig	strange
Eimer *m*	bucket
	pail
einfach	easy
einfetten	grease, to
einhalten (z.B. Vorschriften)	comply with, to
Einhandhobel *m*	block plane
Einhandzwinge *f*	one-hand clamp
Einhieb *m*	single-cut
Einhieb-Feile *f*	single-cut file
Einlasseckenhobel *m*	mortise plane
Einmalhandschuh *m*	medical glove
	one-way glove
einseitig	single-faced
Einweiser *m* (z.B. Kran, LKW)	banksman
Einzelheit *f*	detail
Eis *nsg*	ice *sg*
Eisen *n*	iron
Eisenguss *m*	iron casting
Eisensäge *f*	hacksaw
Elektrikermeißel *m*	electrician's chisel
Elektrikerschlitzmeißel *m*	electrician's splitting chisel
elektrisch	electric
Elektronikzange *f*	electronic pliers *pl*
elektronischer Digital-Messschieber *m*	electronic digtal caliper

E

empfindlich	sensitive
Engländer *m*	adjustable spanner *(BE)*
	adjustable wrench *(BE)*
	crescent wrench *(AE)*
	monkey wrench *(AE)*
Englischer Klauenhammer *m*	claw hammer, English pattern
entgegen allen Erwartungen	against all odds
Entleerungsventil *n*	drain valve
entsprechen (z.B. Bedingungen)	comply with, to
entzündlich	flammable
Erdgas *n*	natural gas
erforderlich	necessary
erfüllen (z.B. Frist)	comply with, to
ernst	serious
Ersatzblatt *n*	replacement blade
Ersatzteil *n*	spare part
Eschenstiel *m*	ash handle
Estrich *m*	screed
Etage *f*	floor
Exzenterschleifer *m*	random orbital sander

F

Fabrik *f*	factory
Fahrenheit *n*	Fahrenheit
fahrlässig	careless
Fahrstuhl *m*	elevator *(AE)* (lift)
	lift *(BE)*
Falzhobel *m*	fillister plane
	rabbet plane *(AE)*
	rebate plane *(BE)*
Farbe *f*	paint
farbiger Beton *m*	coloured concrete

Farbroller *m*	paint roller
Farbtopf *m*	paint can
Farbverdünner *m*	paint thinner
Farbwanne *f*	paint tray
Fasenhobel *m*	chamfer plane
Fass *n*	barrel
Fasskarre *f*	drum trolley
Fassschaber *m*	barrel draw knife
Fassschlüssel *m*	bung wrench
faul	lazy
Fäustel *m*	club hammer
	lump hammer
Fax *m/n*	fax
Faxnummer *f*	fax number
Februar *m*	February
Federstahl *m*	spring steel
Federzwinge *f*	spring clamp
Fehlerbeschreibung *f*	defect description
Feiertag *m*	holiday
Feile *f*	file
feiner Riss *m*	hairline crack
Feinsäge *f*	gent's saw
Feinsägefeile *f*	saw file for gent's saw
Feinstabziehstein *m*	fine honing stone
Fenster kippen	tilt a window, to
Fenster *n*	window
Fensterkitt *m*	window putty
Fensterrahmen *m*	window frame
fest	tight
fester Bügel *m*	fixed bow
festgelegt	specified

F

Festklemmzange *f*	gripping pliers *pl* locking pliers *pl*
Feststellzange *f*	gripping pliers *pl* locking pliers *pl*
Fettpresse *f*	grease gun lubrication gun
Feuchtigkeit *fsg*	moisture *sg*
feuchtigkeitsbeständig	moisture-proof
feuchtigkeitsempfindlich	moisture-sensitive
feuchtigkeitsresistent	moisture-proof
Feuerlöschdecke *f*	fire blanket
Feuerlöscher *m*	fire extinguisher
Fidibushobel *m*	spill plane
Firnis *m*	varnish
Flachdechsel *m*	flat adz *(AE)* flat adze *(BE)*
Flächenhobel *m*	bench plane
Flachfeile *f*	flat file
Flachlineal *n*	straight edge
Flachmeißel *m*	flat chisel
Flachpinsel *m*	flat brush
Flachrundzange *f*	flat round pliers *pl*
Flachzange *f*	flat pliers *pl* flat-nose pliers *pl*
Flaschenhalterung *f*	cylinder rack
Flechterzange *f*	concrete pliers *pl* concretor's pliers *pl* mechanic's nippers *pl* monier pliers *pl* Rabitz pliers *pl*
fleißig	diligent
Flex *f* (® FLEX Elektrowerkzeuge GmbH)	angle grinder disc grinder

F

flexibel	flexible
flexible Dübelsäge *f*	flush cutting saw
Fliese *f*	tile
Fliesenbrechzange *f*	tile breaking pl ers *pl*
Fliesenhammer *m*	tile hammer
Fliesenkeil *m*	tile wedge
Fliesenkleber *m*	tile adhesive
Fliesenlegerkelle *f*	tiler's trowel
Fliesenlochschneider *m*	tile hole cutter
Fliesenmeißel *m*	tile chisel
Fliesenschneid- und Brechzange *f*	tile cutting and breaking pliers *pl*
Fliesenschneidemaschine *f*	tile cutting machine
Fliesenschwamm *m*	tile sponge
Flugasche *f*	fly ash
Flügelschraube *f*	wing screw
Flüssigkeit *f*	liquid
Formaldehyd *msg/nsg*	formaldehyde *sg*
Forstnerbohrer *m*	Forstner bit
	Forstner drill
Fräse *f*	milling machine
Fräsmaschine *f*	milling machine
Freitag *m*	Friday
freundlich	friendly
Frischbeton *m*	fresh concrete
frühe Morgenstunden *fpl*	small hours *pl*
Frühstückspause *f*	morning break
Fuchsschwanz *m*	handsaw
Fugenkelle *f*	joint trowel
Fugenmeißel *m*	brick cutting chisel
	jointing chisel
Fugenpistole *f*	caulkir g gun

F

Fühlerlehre *f*	feeler gauge
Füllspachtel *f*/*m*	filling knife
Fünfeck *n*	pentagon
Funktionsprüfung *f*	functional testing
Furnier *n*	veneer
Furnierhammer *m*	veneer hammer
Furniersäge *f*	veneer saw
Furnierschabhobel *m*	cabinet scraper
Furnierschneider *m*	veneer cutter
Fußbodenheizung *f*	underfloor heating

G

Gafferband *n*	gaffer tape
galvanisiert	galvanized
Ganzstahlzwinge *f*	all-steel screw clamp
Gas *n*	gas
Gasbeton *m*	autoclaved aerated concrete/AAC autoclaved cellular concrete/ACC autoclaved lightweight concrete/ALC
Gasflasche *f*	gas cylinder
Gasmelder *m*	gas detector
gebogen	bent
Gebotszeichen *n*	mandatory sign
Gebrauchsanleitung *f*	user guide user manual
gefährlich	dangerous
gefährlicher Abfall *m*	hazardous waste
gegen alle Schwierigkeiten	against all odds
gehärtet	hardened
Gehörschutz *m*	ear protection

G

Gehrmaß n	miter square (AE)
	mitre square (BE)
Gehrung f	miter (AE)
	mitre (BE)
Gehrungssäge f	miter saw (AE)
	mitre saw (BE)
Gehrungsschablone f	miter saddle (AE)
	mitre saddle (BE)
Gehrungsschneidlade f	miter box (AE)
	mitre box (BE)
Gehrungswinkel m	miter square (AE)
	mitre square (BE)
gekröpft	swan neck shape
	offset
genau	exact
	precise
gerade	straight
gerader Schlichtstahl m	square end scraper
geräuscharm	low-noise
gereinigt	cleaned
Geruch m	odor (AE)
	odour (BE)
geruchsneutral	odor-free (AE)
	odour-free (BE)
Gerüst n	scaffolding
Geschäftsräume mpl	business premises pl
	office premises pl
	premises pl
geschätzt	roughly
Gestellsäge f	frame saw
gestern	yesterday
Gewicht n	weight
Gewinde n	thread
Gewindestange f	threaded rod

G

Gewindestrehler *m*	thread chaser
Giftmüll *msg*	hazardous waste
Gips *m*	gypsum
Gipsbecher *m*	plaster mixing bowl
Gipserbeil *n*	drywall hammer
Gipserhammer *m*	drywall hammer
Gipserspachtel *f/m*	plasterer's spatula
Gipskarton-Bauplatte/GKB *f*	sheetrock (® United States Gypsum Company) *(AE)* plasterboard *(BE)* gypsum plasterboard *(BE)* drywall *(AE)* gypsum board *(AE)* gypsum wallboard *(AE)* wallboard *(AE)*
Gipskartonplatte/GKP *f*	sheetrock (® United States Gypsum Company) *(AE)* plasterboard *(BE)* gypsum plasterboard *(BE)* drywall *(AE)* gypsum board *(AE)* gypsum wallboard *(AE)* wallboard *(AE)*
Gipsplatte *f*	gypsum plasterboard plasterboard
Gipswandbauplatte *f*	sheetrock (® United States Gypsum Company) *(AE)* plasterboard *(BE)* gypsum plasterboard *(BE)* drywall *(AE)* gypsum board *(AE)* gypsum wallboard *(AE)* wallboard *(AE)*
glänzend	glossy
Glaspapier *n*	glass paper
Glasschneider *m*	glass cutter

G

German	English
Glaswolle *f*	glass wool
glatte Bahn *f* (glatte Schlagfläche)	plain face
Glättekelle *f*	smoothing trowel
Gliedermaßstab *m*	folding rule
Grad *m*	degree
Gradmesser *m*	protractor
Gradmesser mit halbrunder Grundplatte *m*	protractor with halfround head
Gradmesser mit rechteckiger Grundplatte *m*	protractor with rectangular head
Granit *m*	granite
Graphit *m*	graphite
Grat *m*	burr
Grathobel *m*	dovetail plane
Gratsäge *f*	stair saw
Gratzieher *m*	scraper burnisher
Graupel *f*	graupel sleet
Griesel *msg*	snow grains *pl*
Gripzange *f*	gripping pliers *pl* locking pliers *pl*
grob	roughly
groß	1. big (volume/mass) 2. tall (height) 3. large (area)
Größe *f*	size
Grundeisen *n*	bottom cleaning chisel
Grundhobel *m*	router plane
Gully *m/n*	storm drain storm sewer *(AE)* drain
Gummihalter *m*	rubber holder
Gummihammer *m*	rubber mallet

G

Gummihandschuh *m*	rubber glove
Gummistiefel *m*	rubber boot Wellington boot
Gussstahl *m*	cast steel
gut	good
Gut gemacht!	Well done!
gute Arbeit leisten	do a good job, to

H

Haarlineal *n*	straight edge
Haarwinkel *m*	beveled steel square *(AE)* bevelled steel square *(BE)*
Hagel *msg*	hail
Haken *m*	hook
halbrund (mittel)	half-round (middle)
Halbrundfeile *f*	half round file
halbschlicht (mittel)	half smooth *sg* (middle) cut 2 (middle)
Hammer für Werkzeugmacher *m*	toolmaker's hammer
Hammer *m*	hammer
Hammer zum Justieren von Hobeleisen *m*	blade adjustment hammer
Hammerbügel *m*	hammer holder
Hammerstiel *m*	hammer handle
Handbesen *m*	hand brush
Handfeger *m*	hand brush
Handschaufel *f*	hand-shovel
Handy *n*	cell phone *(AE)* cellular phone *(AE)* mobile phone *(BE)*
Handynummer *f*	cell phone number *(AE)* mobile phone number *(BE)*

Hanfschnur f	hemp cord
Harpuneneisen n	harpoon chisel
hart (Konsistenz)	hard (consistency)
Hartfaserplatte f	hardboard
Hartholz n	hardwood
Hartholzsäge f	hardwood saw
Haspel f/m	reel
hässlich	ugly
Hebelzwinge f	lever clamp
Hebezeug n	hoisting equipment
Heft n	handle
Heftzwecke f	drawing pin (BE)
	pin (BE)
	push pin
	tack (AE)
	thumbtack (AE)
heiß	hot
Heißklebepistole f	hot-glue gun
Heizkörper m	radiator
Heizkörperpinsel m	radiator brush
helfen	help, to
Hersteller m	manufacturer
	producer
Herstellungsjahr n	year of manufacture
heute	today
Hickorystiel m	hickory handle
Hieb 1 m	bastard (coarse)
	cut 1 (coarse)
Hieb 2 m	half smooth sg (middle)
	cut 2 (middle)
Hieb 3 m	cut 3 (fine)
	smooth (fine)
Hieb m	cut

H

hilfsbereit	helpful
hinten	back, at the back
Hitze *fsg*	heat *sg*
Hobel *m*	plane
Hobelbank *f*	joiner's bench
Hobelspäne *mpl*	wood shavings *pl*
hochentzündlich	highly flammable
Hochofenzement *m*	blast furnace slag cement
höflich	polite
Höhe *f*	height
Hohlbeitel *m*	firmer gouge
Hohldechsel *m*	bowl maker's adze *(BE)* hollow adz *(AE)* hollow adze *(BE)*
Hohlkehlhobel *m*	rounding plane
Holzbehandlung *f*	wood treatment
Holzbohrer *m* (Einsatz)	wood bit
Holzdübel *m*	wooden dowel
Holzhammer *m*	mallet
Holzkeil *m*	wooden wedge
Holzleim *m*	wood glue
Holzschraube *f*	wood screw
Holzschutzmittel *n*	wood preservative
Holzspäne *mpl*	wood shavings *pl*
hydraulisch	hydraulic

H

I

Imprägnierung *f*	impregnation
Inbus *m* (® Ruia Group)	allen key (® Allen Manufacturing Company) allen wrench (® Allen Manufacturing Company) hex key
Inbusschlüssel *m* (® Ruia Group)	allen key (® Allen Manufacturing Company) allen wrench (® Allen Manufacturing Company) hex key
industrielles Gas *n*	industrial gas technical gas
Information *f*	information *sg*
informieren	inform, to
Initialen *fpl*	initials *pl*
inkonsequent	inconsistent
Innen-Torx-Schraube *f* (® acument)	internal Torx screw (® acument)
Inneneckenkelle *f*	inner corner trowel
Innensechskant-Schraubendreher *m*	Allen key (® Allen Manufacturing Company) hexagon key hex key
Innensechskantschraube *f*	Allen screw (® Allen Manufacturing Company)
Innentaster *m*	inside caliper
insbesondere	especially
Intarsiensäge *f*	inlay saw
interessant	interesting
Isolierband *n*	electrical tape insulating tape

I

J

Jahr *n*	year
jährlich	annual
Jalousie *f*	Venetian blind
Januar *m*	January
Japanspachtel *f/m*	Japanese spatula
Juli *m*	July
jung	young
Juni *m*	June
Juweliersäge *f*	jeweller's saw
Juweliersägeblatt *n*	jeweller's blade

K

Kabel *n*	cable
Kabelschere *f*	cable shears *pl*
Kabeltrommel *f* (Erdkabel)	cable drum
Kabeltrommel *f* (Verlängerungsleitung)	cable reel
Kalk *m*	lime
Kalkstein *m*	limestone
kalkulieren	calculate, to
kalt	cold
Kaltreiniger *m*	cold cleaner
Kanister *m*	jerry can
Kantenhobel *m*	edge trimmer
Kantholz *n*	squared timber
Kappsäge *f*	chop saw
Kartätsche *f*	cartridge
Kartonschachtel *f*	cardboard box
kegelförmiger Bilderhauer-schleifstein *m*	conical gouge slip stone

Kehrblech *n*	dustpan
Kehrschaufel *f*	dustpan
Kelle *f*	trowel
Kette *f*	chain
Kienspanhobel *m*	spill plane
Kies *m*	gravel
Kilowatt/kW *n*	kilowatt/kW
Kippventil *n*	tilt valve
Kitt *m*	putty
Kittmesser *n*	putty knife
Klappspaten *m*	entrenching tool folding spade
Klarlack *m*	clear coat clear lacquer
Klebeband *n*	adhesive tape
Klebepistole *f*	glue gun
klein	small little
Kleinigkeiten *fpl*	odds and ends *pl (coll.)*
Klimaanlage *f*	air conditioner air conditioning
Klinge *f*	blade
Klingel *f*	bell doorbell
Klinker *m*	clinker
Klopfholz *n*	carpenter's mallet
Klüpfel mit Bronzekopf *m*	bronze-head mallet
Klüpfel mit Eisenkopf *m*	iron-head mallet
Klüpfel mit Messingkopf *m*	brass-head mallet
Knarre *f*	ratchet spanner *(BE)* ratchet wrench *(AE)* socket spanner *(BE)* socket wrench *(AE)*

K

Kneifzange *f*	carpenter's pincers *pl* pincers *pl*
Kniekissen *n*	knee cushion
Knieschoner *m*	knee pad
Kohlenstoffstahl *m*	carbon steel
Kollege *m*	colleague
Kombinationswinkel *m*	combination square
Kombischleifstein *m*	combination stone
Kombizange *f*	combi pliers *pl* comb pliers *pl* combination pliers *pl*
Kommunikation *f*	communication
konsequent	consistent
Kontaktdaten *pl*	contact details *pl*
Kontrollwinkel *m*	control square
Konturschablone *f*	profile gauge
Kork *m*	cork
Korkboden *m*	cork flooring
Körner *m*	center punch *(AE)* centre punch *(BE)*
Körnung *f*	grain
Korpus *m*	body
Korpuszwinge *f*	body clamp
Korrekturpulver *n*	correction powder
korrodiert	corroded
Kraft-Kombizange *f*	high-leverage combi pliers *pl* high-leverage comb pliers *pl* high-leverage combination pliers *pl*
Kraftseitenschneider *m*	high-leverage diagonal cutter
Kranarbeiten *fpl*	crane work *sg*
Kranführer *m*	crane driver crane operator

K

Kranführerschein *m*	crane driver licence *(BE)*
	crane driver's license *(AE)*
	crane operator licence *(BE)*
	crane operator's license *(AE)*
Kreide *f*	chalk
Kreis *m*	circle
Kreissäge *f*	buzz saw *(AE)*
	circular saw *(BE)*
Kreppband *n*	masking tape
Kreuzhieb *m*	cross-cut
	double-cut
Kreuzhieb-Feile *f*	cross-cut file
	double-cut file
Kreuzmeißel *m*	cross-cut chisel
Kreuzschlitzschraube *f*	Phillips screw
	(® Phillips Screw Company)
Kreuzschlitzschraubendreher *m*	Phillips screwdriver
	(® Phillips Screw Company)
Kreuzschlüssel *m*	lug wrench *(AE)*
	wheel brace *(BE)*
	wheel wrench *(BE)*
Krimskrams *msg (ugs.)*	odds and ends *pl (coll.)*
Kugelhammer *m*	ball peen hammer *(AE)*
	ball pein hammer *(BE)*
Kuhfuß *m*	crowbar
	pry bar
	wrecking bar
Kunde *m*	client
Kunststoff *m*	plastic
Kunststoffhammer *m*	plastic hammer
	plastic mallet
Kunststoffmaßband *n*	plastic measuring tape
Kunststoffsäge *f*	plastic saw
Kupfer *nsg*	copper *sg*

K

Kupferhammer *m*	copper hammer
Kurzbeitel *m*	butt chisel
kurzfristig	short-term

L

Lack *m*	varnish
Laminat *n*	laminate
Laminatboden *m*	laminate flooring
Laminierwalze *f*	laminating roller
Länge *f*	length
langfristig	long-term
langsam	slow
Längsschnitt *m*	ripcut
langweilig	boring
Laser *m*	laser
Latexfarbe *f*	latex paint
Latthammer *m*	carpenter's roofing hammer roofing hammer
Latzhose *f*	dungarees *pl (BE)* bib overalls *pl (AE)*
Laubsäge *f*	coping saw fret saw
Laubsägeblatt *n*	fretsaw blade
Laubsägetischchchen *n*	fret saw table
laut	loud
Leckage *f*	leakage
Leder *n*	leather
Lederabziehscheibe *f*	leather honing wheel
Lederhammer *m*	rawhide hammer
legierter Stahl *m*	alloyed steel
Lehrgeld zahlen *(ugs.)*	learn the hard way, to *(coll.)*
Lehrgerüst *n*	falsework

L

leicht (Masse)	light (mass)
leicht (mühelos)	easy
Leichtbeton *m*	lightweight concrete
Leimpistole *f*	glue gun
Leinölfirnis *m*	boiled linseed oil
leise	quiet
Leiter *f*	ladder
Lenzpumpe *f*	bilge pump
letzte Woche	last week
letzter Monat	last month
letztes Jahr	last year
Libelle *f*	vial
Lieferant *m*	supplier
	vendor
Lift *m*	elevator *(AE)* (ift)
	lift *(BE)*
Lineal *n*	ruler (tool)
linke	left
links	left
	left, on the
Linoleum *nsg*	linoleum *sg*
Linoleummesser *n*	linoleum knife
Lochaxt *f*	mortise ax *(AE)*
	mortise axe *(BE)*
	mortising ax *(AE)*
	mortising axe *(BE)*
Lochbeitel *m*	mortise chisel
Locheisen *n*	hollow punch
Lochsäge *f*	hole cutter
	hole saw
Lochzange *f*	hole punch pliers *pl*
Löschdecke *f*	fire blanket

L

Lösungsmittel *n*	solvent
Lötkolben *m*	soldering iron
Lötzinn *nsg*	tin solder *sg*
Luft *fsg*	air *sg*
Luftfeuchte *fsg*	air moisture *sg* humidity
Luftfeuchtigkeit *fsg*	air moisture *sg* humidity
Lupe *f*	magnifying glass

M

Magnet *m*	magnet
magnetische Sägeführung *f*	magnetic saw guide
Mai *m*	May
Malerkrepp *m*	masking tape
Malerrolle *f*	paint roller
Malerspachtel *f/m*	scraper spackle knife painter's spatula
Malerwalze *f*	paint roller
Manometer *n*	manometer pressure gauge
markieren	mark, to
Markierung *f*	mark marking
März *m*	March
Maschine *f*	machine
Maschinenhülle *f*	machine cover
Maschinenschraube *f*	machine screw
Maßband *n*	measuring tape tape measure
Maßstab *m*	ruler (tool)

matt	matt
Mauerstein *m*	brick
Maurerhammer *m*	brick mason's hammer
	bricklayer's hammer
	mason's hammer
Maurerkelle *f*	trowel
Maurermeißel *m*	bricklayer's chisel
Maurerschnur *f*	cord
	string line
MDF-Platte *f*	medium-density fibreboard/MDF
mechanisch	mechanical
Mehrzwecksäge *f*	multipurpose saw
Meißel *m*	chisel
merkwürdig	strange
Messbecher *m*	measuring cup
Messer *n*	knife
Messerfeile *f*	knife file
Messing *n*	brass
Messingbürste *f*	brass brush
Messinghammer *m*	brass hammer
Messkeil *m*	measuring wedge
Messschieber *m*	caliper
Messung *f*	measurement
Messwert *m*	measurement
Metallfass *n*	metal drum
Metallschaber *m*	metal scraper
Meterstab *m*	folding rule
mieten	rent, to
Mikrometer *n*	outside micrometer *(AE)*
	outside micrometre *(BE)*
Mikrometerschraube *f*	outside micrometer *(AE)*
	outside micrometre *(BE)*

mineralisch	mineral
Mineralwolle *f*	mineral wool
Mini-Feinsäge *f*	mini gent's saw
mit etwas in Konflikt stehen	odds with something, to be at
mit jemandem uneinig sein	odds with somebody, to be at
mit jemandem uneins sein	odds with somebody, to be at
mit sich selbst uneins sein	odds with oneself, to be at
Mittag *m*	noon
Mittagspause *f*	lunch break
mitteldichte Faserplatte/MDF *f*	medium-density fibreboard/MDF
mitteldichte Holzfaserplatte/MDF *f*	medium-density fibreboard/MDF
Mittelpunktfinder *m*	center finder *(AE)*
	centre finder *(BE)*
Mittwoch *m*	Wednesday
Mobilnummer *f*	cell phone number *(AE)*
	mobile phone number *(BE)*
Mobiltelefon *n*	cell phone *(AE)*
	cellular phone *(AE)*
	mobile phone *(BE)*
Mobiltelefonnummer *f*	cell phone number *(AE)*
	mobile phone number *(BE)*
Monat *m*	month
monatlich	monthly
Monierzange *f*	concrete pliers *pl*
	concretor's pliers *pl*
	mechanic's nippers *pl*
	monier pliers *pl*
	Rabitz pliers *pl*
Montag *m*	Monday
Montage *f*	installation
Montagearbeit *f*	installation work
Montagesatz *m*	mounting set
morgen	tomorrow

Morgen *m*	morning
Mörtel *m*	mortar
Mörtelkübel *m*	mortar tub
Mörtelspritzmaschine *f*	mortar gun
Motoröl *n*	engine oil
müde	tired
Mulde *f*	skip
Muldencontainer *m*	skip
Mutter *f* (Werkzeug)	nut

N

Nachmittag *m*	afternoon
nächste Woche	next week
nächster Monat	next month
nächstes Jahr	next year
Nacht *f*	night
Nadel *f*	needle
Nadelfeile *f*	needle file
Nagel *m*	nail
Nagelbohrer *m*	gimlet
Nageleisen *n*	crowbar
	nail puller
	pry bar
	wrecking bar
Nagelsenker *m*	nail punch
Nageltreiber *m*	nail punch
Nagelversenker *m*	nail punch
Nagelzieher *m*	nail puller
Nagurastein *m*	nagura stone
Nähahle *f*	sewing awl
Nähmaschinenöl *n*	sewing machine oil

0

nass	wet
Nassschleifmaschine f	wet grinding wheel
Neigungsmessgerät n	slant level
Netz n	net
neugierig	curious
Newtonmeter/Nm m/n	newton metre/Nm (BE) newton meter/Nm (AE)
nicht brennbar	non-flammable
nicht erforderlich	unnecessary
nichts für ungut (ugs.)	no hard feelings pl (coll.)
Nickel nsg	nickel sg
Niesel m	drizzle
Nieselregen m	drizzle
Norm f	standard
Normalbeton m	concrete
notwendig	necessary
November m	November
Nuss f	socket
Nutenmeißel m	grooving chisel
Nuthobel m	plough plane (BE) plow plane (AE)
Nylonhammer m	nylon hammer

O

oben	top, on the
oberste	top
oberster	top
oberstes	top
offene Flamme f	naked flame
offenes Licht n	naked light
Ohrenschützer fpl	ear protection

Ohrenstöpsel *m*	ear plug
Ohrstöpsel *m*	ear plug
Oktober *m*	October
Öl *n*	oil
Ölkanne *f*	oil can
Ölstein *m*	oil stone
Ortbeton *m*	in-situ concrete
oval	oval
ovaler Drehstahl *m*	oval skew chisel
Ovalpinsel *m*	oval shaped brush

P

Packbandabroller *m*	tape gun
Paneele *f*	panel
Panzerband *n*	duck tape
	duct tape
Pappkarton *m (ugs.)*	cardboard box
Parallel-Schraubzwinge *f*	hand screw clamp
	parallel clamp
Parkett *n*	parquet
Parkettboden *m*	parquet flooring
Pferdestärke/PS *f*	horsepower/hp
Pflasterhammer *m*	paving hammer
Pfosten *m*	post
Phasenprüfer *m*	mains tester
Pinsel *m*	brush
Pinselreiniger *m*	brush cleaner
Pinzette *f*	tweezers *pl*
Plane *f*	tarpaulin
pneumatisch	pneumatic
Pockholz *n*	lignum vitae

P

Polier *m*	foreman
Porenbeton *m*	autoclaved aerated concrete/AAC autoclaved cellular concrete/ACC autoclaved lightweight concrete/ ALC
Porenbetonsäge *f*	cellular concrete saw
Portlandhüttenzement *m*	Portland slag cement
Portlandkalksteinzement *m*	Portland limestone cement
Portlandkompositzement *m*	Portland composite cement
Portlandzement *m*	Portland cement
Portlandzementklinker *m*	Portland cement clinker
Pozidriv-Schraubendreher *m* (® Phillips Screw Company)	Pozidriv screwdriver (® Phillips Screw Company)
Pozidrivschraube *f* (® Phillips Screw Company)	Pozidriv screw (® Phillips Screw Company)
präzise	precise
Präzisionsschmiege *f*	precision sliding bevel
Präzisionswinkel *m*	precision try square
Präzisionswinkel mit Gehrung *m*	precision try square with miter *(AE)* precision try square with mitre *(BE)*
Preis *m*	price
Priorität *f*	priority
Problem *n*	problem
Profilabtaster *m*	profile gauge
Profillehre *f*	profile gauge
Profilschablone *f*	profile gauge
Profiltiefenmesser *m*	tire tread depth gauge *(AE)* tyre tread depth gauge *(BE)*
Projekt *n*	project
Projektleiter *m*	project manager
Pulver *n*	powder
Pumpe *f*	pump

pünktlich	punctually
pünktlich (auf den Punkt)	on time
punktschweißen	weld-spot, to
Putzhobel *m*	smoothing plane

Q

Qualität *f*	quality
Quast *m*	broad brush
Querbeil *n*	adz *(AE)*
	adze *(BE)*
Querschnitt *m*	crosscut

R

Rabitzzange *f*	concrete pliers *pl*
	concretor's pliers *pl*
	mechanic's nippers *pl*
	monier pliers *pl*
	Rabitz pliers *pl*
Radio *n*	radio
Radiozange *f*	radio pliers *pl*
Radius *m*	radius
Radkreuz *n*	lug wrench *(AE)*
	wheel brace *(BE)*
	wheel wrench *(BE)*
Radlader *m*	wheel loader
	wheeled loader
Rahmen *m*	frame
Rahmenspanner *m*	corner clamp
Raspel *f*	rasp
Raspelhieb *m*	rasp cut
Ratsche *f*	ratchet spanner *(BE)*
	ratchet wrench *(AE)*
	socket spanner *(BE)*
	socket wrench *(AE)*

R

Raubank *f*	jointer plane
Rauchen *nsg*	smoking
Rauchmelder *m*	smoke detector
Rauchverbot *n*	smoking ban
Rauhbank *f*	jointer plane
rauhe Bahn *f* (gekerbte Schlagfläche)	checked face
Räumahle *f*	reamer
Räumer *m*	reamer
Raureif *msg*	hoarfrost
rechte	right
rechteckig	rectangular
rechter Winkel *m*	right angle
rechts	right right, on the
rechtzeitig (nicht auf den Punkt)	in time
Regen *m*	rain
Reibahle *f*	reamer
Reibebrett *n*	float
Reifenluftdruckmesser *m*	tire pressure gauge *(AE)* tyre pressure gauge *(BE)*
Reisigbesen *m*	besom
Reißnadel *f*	scriber stabbing awl
Reißnagel *m*	drawing pin *(BE)* pin *(BE)* push pin tack *(AE)* thumbtack *(AE)*
Reißzwecke *f*	drawing pin *(BE)* pin *(BE)* push pin tack *(AE)* thumbtack *(AE)*

R

Reklamation f	complaint
Reparatur f	repair
reparieren	repair, to
Rettungsleiter f	rescue ladder
Revolverlochzange f	revolving punch pliers pl
Rheinischer Maurerhammer m	mason's hammer, Rhenish type
Richtscheit m	straight edge
Rigipsplatte f (® Saint-Gobain Rigips GmbH)	sheetrock (® United States Gypsum Company) (AE) plasterboard (BE) gypsum plasterboard (BE) drywall (AE) gypsum board (AE) gypsum wallboard (AE) wallboard (AE)
Ring m	ring
Ringeisen n	ring tool
Ringpinsel m	ring brush
Ringschneider m	captive ring tool
Riss m	crack
Rockwolle f (® Rockwool)	rock wool (® Rockwool)
Rohhauthammer m	rawhide hammer
Rohrabschneider m	pipe cutter
Rohrschelle f	pipe clamp pipe clip
Rohrschneider m	pipe cutter
Rohrschraubstock m	pipe vice (BE) pipe vise (AE)
Rohrzange f	pipe wrench
Rohrzwinge f	pipe clamp
Rollgabelschlüssel m	adjustable spanner (BE) adjustable wrench (BE) crescent wrench (AE) monkey wrench (AE)

R

Rollgerüst *n*	mobile scaffold rolling scaffold
Rolltasche *f*	tool roll
Rost *m*	rust
rostfrei	stainless
Rostradierer *m*	rust eraser
Rückensäge *f*	carcass saw *(AE)*
Rücksäge *f*	back saw
rückwärts	backwards *(BE)* backward *(AE)*
rund	round
runder Diamantschleifer *m*	round diamond sharpener
runder Schrotstahl *m*	round nose scraper
Rundfeile *f*	round file
Rundkelle *f*	round trowel
Rundprofil *n*	round profile
Rundprofileisen *n*	bead forming tool
Rundstabhobel *m*	hollow plane
Rüttelplatte *f*	vibratory plate

S

Säbelsäge *f*	reciprocating saw
Sack *m*	sack
Sackkarre *f*	dolly *(AE)* (tool) hand truck *(AE)* sack barrow sack truck *(BE)*
Säge *f*	saw
Sägeangel *f*	saw blade holder
Sägeblatt *n*	saw blade
Sägeblattaufnahme *f*	saw blade holder
Sägeblatthalter *m*	saw blade holder
Sägebock *m* (A-Form)	sawhorse

Sägebock *m* (X-Form)	sawbuck
Sägefeile *f*	saw file
Sägeführung *f*	saw guide
Sägegriff *m*	saw handle
Sägespäne *mpl*	wood shavings *pl*
Salamitaktik *f (ugs.)*	salami tactics *pl (coll.)*
Salzsäure *f*	hydrochloric acid
Samstag *m*	Saturday
Sand *m*	sand
sauber	clean
Säure *f*	acid
säurebeständig	acid-proof
	acid-resistant
Säuredichte *f*	acid density
säurefrei	acid-free
säureresistent	acid-proof
	acid-resistant
Schaber *m*	hand scraper
	scraper
	square end scraper
Schabhobel *m*	spokeshave
Schäkel *m*	shackle
Schälbeitel *m*	paring chisel
Schäleisen *n*	bark spud
Schalenröhre *f*	bowl gouge
Schalenschlichtstahl *m*	bowl finishing tool
Schallpegel *m*	sound level
	decibel level
Schalung *f*	formwork
	casing
schärfen	sharpen, to
Schärfhilfe *f*	honing guide
scharfkantig	sharp-edged
Schärfstein *m*	sharpening stone

S

Schärfsteinabrichtblock *m* (Siliziumkarbid)	flattening stone
Schärfsteinabrichtblock *m* (Stahl)	lapping plate
Schärfsteinhalter *m*	whetstone holder
Scharnier *n*	hinge
Schaufel *f*	shovel
Schaum *m*	foam
Schellack *m*	shellac
Schere *f*	scissors *pl*
Schieblehre *f*	caliper
Schiffshobel *m*	compass plane
schimmelig	moldy *(AE)* mouldy *(BE)*
Schindelspalthacke *f*	froe
Schinder *m*	spokeshave
Schippe *f*	shovel
Schittersäge *f*	bow saw
Schittersägeblatt *n*	bow saw blade
Schlagbohrmaschine *f*	hammer drill
Schlagschnur *f*	chalk line
Schlauch *m*	hose
Schlauchbinder *m*	hose clamp hose clip
Schlauchschelle *f*	hose clamp hose clip
schlecht	bad
schlechte Arbeit	poor work
Schleifführung *f*	honing guide
Schleifklotz *m*	sanding block
Schleifmaschine *f*	sharpening machine
Schleifpapier *n*	sandpaper
Schleifpaste *f*	sharpening paste
Schleifscheibe *f*	grinding wheel

S

Schleifstab *m*	grinding stick
schlicht (fein)	cut 3 (fine)
	smooth (fine)
Schlichthobel *m*	jack plane
Schlitz und Zapfen	mortise and tenon
Schlitzbeitel *m*	scabbard chisel
Schlitzmeißel *m*	splitting chisel
Schlitzsäge *f*	rip saw
	sash saw
Schlitzsägeblatt *n*	rip cut blade
Schlitzschraube *f*	slotted screw
Schlitzschraubendreher *m*	slotted screwdriver
Schlosserhammer *m*	machinist's hammer
	cross pein hammer *(BE)*
	cross peen hammer *(AE)*
Schlosserhammer, deutsche Form *m*	machinist's hammer, German pattern
	cross pein hammer, German pattern *(BE)*
	cross peen hammer, German pattern *(AE)*
Schlosserhammer, englische Form *m*	machinist's hammer, English pattern
	cross pein hammer, English patterr *(BE)*
	cross peen hammer, English patterr *(AE)*
Schlüssel *m*	key
Schlüsselfeile *f*	key file
	warding file
Schmiedehammer *m*	blacksmith's hammer
Schmiege *f*	sliding bevel
schmieren	grease, to
Schmierpresse *f*	grease gun
	lubrication gur
Schmirgelpapier *n*	sandpaper

S

Schmutz *msg*	dirt *sg*
schmutzempfindlich	dirt-sensitive
schmutzig	dirty
Schnee *msg*	snow *sg*
Schneefall *m*	snowfall
Schneematsch *msg*	slush *sg*
Schneidenschutz für Stemmeisen *m*	chisel edge guard
Schneidkluppe *f*	die stock
Schneidlade *f*	miter box *(AE)* mitre box *(BE)*
schnell	fast
Schnellspannbohrfutter *n*	keyless drill chuck
schön	beautiful
schräg angeschliffener Flachstahl *m*	skew chisel
Schrägbeitel *m*	skew chisel
Schragen *m* (X-Form)	sawbuck
Schränkzange *f*	saw set pliers *pl*
Schraube *f*	screw
Schraubendreher *m*	screwdriver
Schraubenschlüssel *m*	spanner *(BE)* wrench *(AE)*
Schraubschelle *f*	screw clamp
Schraubstock *m*	vice *(BE)* vise *(AE)*
Schraubzwinge *f*	screw clamp
Schreinerhammer, französische Form *m*	cabinetmaker's hammer, French pattern
Schreinerhammer *m*	cabinetmaker's hammer
Schreinerklüpfel *m*	cabinetmaker's mallet wood joiner's mallet
Schrott *m*	scrap scrap metal

S

schruppen	grind, to
Schrupphobel *m*	scrub plane
Schruppröhre *f*	roughing out gouge
Schruppstein *m*	coarse stone
Schubkarre *f*	wheelbarrow
Schüppe *f*	shovel
Schuppen *m*	shed
Schusterhammer *m*	cobbler's hammer shoe hammer
Schuttmulde *f*	skip
Schutzbrille *f*	safety glasses *pl* goggles *pl*
Schutzhandschuh *m*	protective glove
Schutzhelm *m*	hard hat
Schutzkleidung *f*	protective clothing
Schwalbenschwanzsäge *f*	dovetail saw
Schwamm drüber *(ugs.)*	no hard feelings *pl (coll.)*
Schwamm *m*	sponge
Schwammbrett *n*	sponge float
Schwanenhals *m*	goose neck swan neck
Schwanenhals-Lochbeitel *m*	swan neck chisel
Schwarzarbeit *f*	moonlighting
Schwedenzange *f*	pipe wrench
Schweifhobel *m*	spokeshave
Schweifsäge *f*	turning bow saw
Schweifsägeblatt *n*	turning saw blade
Schweißabbrand *m*	welding loss
schweißen	weld, to
Schweißer *m*	welder
Schweißerbrille *f*	welding goggles *pl*
Schweißergamasche *f*	welders gaiter
Schweißergebnis *n*	welding result

S

Schweißerhandschuh *m*	welding glove
Schweißerschürze *f*	welding apron
Schweißerzange *f*	welding grip pliers *pl*
Schweißhelm *m*	welding helmet
Schweißmaschine *f*	welding machine
Schweißnaht *f*	weld seam
Schweißpunkt *m*	weld spot
schwer (Masse)	heavy
schwer	difficult
	hard
Schwerbeton *m*	heavyweight concrete
Schwertfeile *f*	slitting file
schwierig	difficult
	hard
Schwingschleifer *m*	orbital sander
Sechseck *n*	hexagon
Seil *n*	rope
Seite *f*	side
Seitenfalzhobel *m*	side rabbet plane *(AE)*
	side rebate plane *(BE)*
Seitenschneider *m*	diagonal cutter
	side cutter
selbstklebendes Maßband *n*	self-adhesive measuring tape
selbstverdichtender Beton/SVB *m*	self-compacting concrete/SCC
seltsam	strange
Senkblei *n*	plumb bob
Senker *m*	countersink
Senklot *n*	blumb bob
	plumb bob
Senklotschnur *f*	plumb bob cord
September *m*	September
Sicheleisen *n*	sickle chisel

S

Sicherheitsschuh *m*	protective shoe
	safety shoe
Sicherheitsventil *n*	safety valve
Sicherheitszeichen *n*	safety sign
Sicherungsringzange *f*	circlip pliers *pl*
Sicherungsringzange für Außenringe *f*	circlip pliers for external rings *pl*
Sicherungsringzange für Innenringe *f*	circlip pliers for internal rings *pl*
Sichtbeton *m*	fair faced concrete
Sichtprüfung *f*	visual inspection
Sickenhammer *m*	bordering hammer
Sieb *n*	sieve
Silikonkarbidpulver *n*	silicon carbide powder
Siliziumkarbid *n*	silicon carbide
Simshobel *m*	fillister plane
	rabbet plane *(AE)*
	rebate plane *(BE)*
Skalierung *f*	graduation
	scaling
Skalpell *n*	scalpel
Solarzelle *f*	solar cell
Sonderabfall *m*	hazardous waste
Sondermüll *msg*	hazardous waste
Sonne *f*	sun
Sonneneinstrahlung *f*	solar radiation
Sonntag *m*	Sunday
Sonntagsarbeit *f*	Sunday work
sorgfältig	careful
	diligent
Spannbeton *m*	prestressed concrete
spannend	exciting

S

Spanplattenschraube *f*	chipboard screw
Spannsäge *f*	frame saw
Spanplatte *f*	chipboard
Spatel *f/m*	scoopula
Spaten *m*	spade
Spaxschraube *f* (® Altenloh, Brinck & Co GmbH & Co. KG)	Spax screw (® Altenloh, Brinck & Co GmbH & Co. KG)
Sperrholz *n*	plywood
Sperrholzboden *m*	plywood floor
speziell	especially specially
spitz	pointed
Spitzhacke *f*	pickax *(AE)* pickaxe *(BE)*
Spitzhammer *m*	pick hammer
Spitzmeißel *m*	pointed chisel
Spitzzange *f*	long-nose pliers *pl* needle-nose pliers *pl* pinch-nose pliers *pl* snipe-nose pliers *pl*
Spitzzirkel *m*	spring type divider
Splintentreiber *m*	pin punch
Splinttreiber *m*	pin punch
Spraydose *f*	aerosol can
spritzwasserdicht	spray-tight
Sprühdose *f*	aerosol can
Sprühflasche *f*	spray bottle
Spülhände *fpl (ugs.)*	dishpan hands *pl (coll.)*
Stachelroller *m*	spike roller
Stahl *m*	steel
Stahl-Anschlagwinkel *m*	steel square
Stahlbeton *m*	reinforced concrete

S

Stahlblech *n*	sheet steel
Stahlfaserbeton *m*	steel fibre reinforced concrete
Stahlmaßband *n*	steel measuring tape
Stahlmaßstab *m*	steel rule
Stahlwolle *fsg*	steel wool *sg* wire wool *sg*
Standsicherheit *fsg*	steadiness stability
Stange *f*	rod
Stangenzirkelspitzen *fpl*	beam compass heads *pl*
stapeln	stack, to
starr	rigid
Staub *m*	dust
staubempfindlich	dust-sensitive
staubig	dusty
Stechahle *f*	piercing awl
Stechbeitel *m*	chisel
Stechbeitel *m* (leichter)	paring chisel
Stechbeitel mit geschwungener Klinge *m*	cranked paring chisel
Stecheisen *n*	chisel
Stechkarre *f*	dolly *(AE)* (tool) hand truck *(AE)* sack barrow sack truck *(BE)*
Stecknuss *f*	socket
Steckschlüssel *m*	ratchet spanner *(BE)* ratchet wrench *(AE)* socket spanner *(BE)* socket wrench *(AE)*
Steckschlüsseleinsatz *m*	socket
Stein-Präparierer *m*	stone grader
Steinwolle *f*	rock wool (® Rockwool)

S

Stemmaxt *f*	mortise ax *(AE)* mortise axe *(BE)* mortising ax *(AE)* mortising axe *(BE)*
Stemmeisen *n*	chisel crowbar pry bar wrecking bar
Stichaxt *f*	mortise ax *(AE)* mortise axe *(BE)* mortising ax *(AE)* mortising axe *(BE)*
Stichling *m*	keyhole saw
Stichsäge *f*	keyhole saw
Storchschnabelzange *f*	stork beak pliers *pl*
Stoßaxt *f*	mortise ax *(AE)* mortise axe *(BE)* mortising ax *(AE)* mortising axe *(BE)*
Stoßscharre *f*	floor scraper
stramm	tight
Straßenablauf *m*	storm drain storm sewer *(AE)* drain
Straßenbesen *m*	street broom
Streichmaß *n*	marking gauge
Stufenstechbeitel *m*	cranked paring chisel
Stuhlmacher-Ziehklingenschaber *m*	chairmaker's scraper
Stukkateurspachtel *f/m*	plasterer's spatula
Stummelstechbeitel *m*	butt chisel
stumpf	dull
Sturm *m*	storm
Styropor *nsg* (® BASF)	Styrofoam *sg* (® Dow Chemical Company)
Substanz *f*	substance

T

Tag *m*	day
täglich	daily
Tapete *f*	wallpaper
Tapezierbürste *f*	wallpaper brush
Tapeziertisch *m*	paste table
	pasting table
	wallpaper table
Taschenbandmaß *n*	pocket measuring tape
Taschenhobel *m*	pocket plane
Taschenlampe *f*	electric torch *(BE)*
	flashlight *(AE)*
Taschenmessschieber *m*	pocket caliper
Tau *n*	rope
tausend	thousand
technisches Gas *n*	industrial gas
	technical gas
teilsynthetisch	semi-synthetic
Telefax *m/n*	fax
Telefaxnummer *f*	fax number
Telefon *n*	phone
	telephone
Telefonnummer *f*	phone number
	telephone number
Telefonzange *f*	telephone pliers *pl*
Temperatur *f*	temperature
Temperguss-Schraubzwinge *f*	malleable cast iron screw clamp
Teppich *m*	carpet
Teppichmesser *n*	box cutter
Terpentin *m/n*	turpentine
Terpentinersatz *msg*	white spirit
Tiefe *f*	depth

T

Tieflochbohrer *m* (Holzbearbeitung)	shell auger long boring tool
Tiegelzange *f*	crucible tongs *pl*
Tinktur *f*	tincture
Tintenbleistift *m*	indelible pencil
Tintenstift *m*	indelible pencil
Tischlerbeil *n*	carpenter's ax *(AE)* carpenter's axe *(BE)*
Tischlerhammer, französische Form *m*	cabinetmaker's hammer, French pattern
Tischlerhammer *m*	cabinetmaker's hammer
Tischlerklüpfel *m*	cabinetmaker's mallet
Tischlerwinkel *m*	try square
Tischlerwinkel mit Anreißfunktion *m*	try square with additional function for parallel marking
Tischlerzirkel *m*	carpenter's gauge
Toilette *f*	restroom *(AE)* toilet *(BE)*
Tonne *f*	barrel
Torxschraube *f* (® acument)	Torx screw (® acument)
Torxschraubendreher *m* (® acument)	Torx screwdriver (® acument)
Transportbeton *m*	ready-mixed concrete
Trapezklinge *f*	trapezoid blades
Traufe *f*	eaves *pl*
trennen	separate, to
Trennschleifer *m*	angle grinder disc grinder
Trennstemmer *m*	paring chisel
Treppe *f*	stairway stairs *pl*
Treppenbauerbeitel *m*	stairmaker's chisel
Trichter *m*	funnel

T

trocken	dry
trockenes Holz *n*	dry wood
Tropenholz *n*	tropical wood
Tür *f*	door
Türdrücker *m*	door handle
Türklingel *f*	bell doorbell
Türklinke *f*	door handle
Türrahmen *m*	door frame
Türschloss *n*	door lock
Türstopper *m*	door stop door stopper
Typ *m*	type

U

Überdruck *m*	overpressure
Überdruckventil *n*	overpressure valve
übermorgen	day after tomorrow, the *sg*
übernächste Woche	week after next, the *sg*
übernächster Monat	month after next, the *sg*
übernächstes Jahr	year after next, the *sg*
überrascht	surprised
übersehen	overlook, to
überwachen	monitor, to
Uhr *f*	clock
ultrahochfester Beton/UHFB *m*	ultra high strength concrete/UHSC
Umdrehungen pro Minute / 1/min / U/min *fpl (ugs.)*	revolutions per minute/rpm *pl*
Umfang *m*	perimeter
Umfang *m* (nur Kreis)	circumference (only circle)
umlegbarer Griff *m*	reversible handle
Umwelt *fsg*	environment

U

undankbar	ungrateful
unehrlich	dishonest
Unfall *m*	accident
Unfallverhütungsvorschriften/ UVV *fpl*	accident prevention regulations *pl*
unfreundlich	unfriendly
ungefähr	roughly
ungereinigt	uncleaned
unhöflich	rude
uninteressant	uninteresting
Universalsäge *f*	universal saw
unlegierter Stahl *m*	unalloyed steel
Unmenge von etwas *f*	oodles of something *pl (coll.)*
unnötig	unnecessary
unsichtbar	invisible
unten	bottom, at the
Unterdruck *m*	vacuum
Unterdruckventil *n*	vacuum valve
untere	bottom
unterer	bottom
unteres	bottom
Unterlegscheibe *f*	washer
unterschiedlich	different
Unterschrift *f*	signature
Unterweisung *f*	instruction
unvernünftig	unreasonable
unverträglich	incompatible
unvorsichtig	careless
unzuverlässig	unreliable
Urlaub *m*	vacation *(AE)* holidays *pl (BE)*
Ursache *f*	cause

U

V

Vakuum *n*	vacuum
Vakuummeter *n*	vacuum gauge
Vario-Ecke *f*	vario corner
Ventil *n*	valve
verantwortlich sein für etwas	responsible for something, to be
Verbandskasten *m*	first aid box
	first aid kit
verblichen	faded
Verbotszeichen *n*	prohibition sign
	prohibitory sign
verchromt	chrome plated
verdichtet	compressed
Verdünner *m*	thinner
Verdünnungsmittel *n*	thinner
vereinbart	stipulated
vergessen etwas zu tun	forget to do something, to
Verkäufer *m*	vendor
verkupfert	copper plated
Verlängerung *f*	extension
Verlängerungsschnur *f*	extension cord *(AE)*
	extension lead *(BE)*
vermeiden	avoid, to
vermieten	rent out, to
vermutlich	probable
vernickelt	nickel plated
vernünftig	reasonable
verschiebbarer Bügel *m*	adjustable bow
verschieben	delay, to
Verschulden *nsg*	fault
Verspätung *f*	delay
versteckter Nagel *m*	hidden nail

V

verzögern	delay, to
Verzögerung *f*	delay
Vieleck *n*	polygon
Vierkant *m/n*	square
Vierkantfeile *f*	square file
vierzehn Tage *mpl*	fortnight *(BE)*
Vogelzungenfeile *f*	crossing file
Vollgummireifen *m*	solid rubber tire *(AE)*
	solid rubber tyre *(BE)*
vollsynthetisch	fully synthetic
Vorarbeiter *m*	foreman
Vorbohrer *m*	gimlet
vorgestern	day before yesterday, the *sg*
Vorhängeschloss *n*	padlock
vorletzte Woche	week before last, the *sg*
vorletzter Monat	month before last, the *sg*
vorletztes Jahr	year before last, the *sg*
Vormittag *m*	morning
vorne	front, at the
Vorrang *m*	priority
Vorschlaghammer *m*	sledgehammer
vorsichtig	careful
Vorstecher *m*	pricking awl
vorvorgestern	three days ago
vorwärts	forwards *(BE)*
	forward *(AE)*

V

W

Wachs *n*	wax
Waffenöl *n*	gun oil
Wagenheber *m*	jack (tool)
wahrscheinlich	probable
Wand *f*	wall
warm	warm
Warnweste *f*	safety vest
Warrington Hammer *m* (Englischer Tischlerhammer)	Warrington hammer (English pattern cabinetmaker's hammer)
Wartung *f*	maintenance
Wartungsarbeit *f*	maintenance work
wartungsarm	low-maintenance
Wartungsfreundlichkeit *fsg*	maintanability *sg*
Waschbenzin *n*	white spirit
Wasser *n*	water
Wasserdampf *m*	water vapor *(AE)* water vapour *(BE)*
wasserfester Bleistift *m*	indelible pencil
Wasserpumpenzange *f*	groove joint pliers *pl* tongue and groove pliers *pl* water pump pliers *pl*
Wasserstein *m*	waterstone
Wasserwaage *f*	level spirit level
Wasserwaage für Pfosten *f*	post level
Wasserwaagenaufsatz *m*	spirit level unit
WC *n*	restroom *(AE)* toilet *(BE)*
Wegbeschreibung *f*	directions *pl*
weich (Konsistenz)	soft (consistency)
Weichholz *n*	softwood

W

Weife *f*	reel
Weißbuche *f*	hornbeam white beech
Weisung *f*	instruction
Werkbank *f*	workbench
Werkschutz *msg*	factory security service factory security office
Werkstückniederhalter *m*	hold down kit
Werktag *m* (in UK/USA keine Unterscheidung zum Arbeitstag)	business day working day
Werkzeuggürtel *m*	tool belt
Werkzeugkasten *m*	toolbox
Werkzeugkoffer *m*	tool case
Werkzeugschrank *m*	tool chest
Wetter *n*	weather
Wettervorhersage *f*	weather forecast
Wind *m*	wind
Winkel *m*	angle
Winkel *m* (Werkzeug)	square
Winkel mit Gehrung *m*	square with miter *(AE)* square with mitre *(BE)*
Winkel mit verschiebbarem Anschlag *m*	double square
Winkellehre *f*	angle gauge
Winkelmesser *m*	protractor
Winkelschleifer *m*	angle grinder disc grinder
Woche *f*	week
Wochenende *n*	weekend
wöchentlich	weekly
Wolkenbruch *m*	cloudburst

W

Z

zählen	count, to
Zahnhobel *m*	toothed plane
Zange *f*	pliers *pl*
Zangenschlüssel *m*	pliers wrench
Zapfensäge *f*	tenon saw
Zapfenstreichmaß mit 2 Messerrädern *n*	dual marking gauge
Zapfenstreichmaß *n*	marking gauge
Zeitarbeit *f*	temporary work temporary employment
Zeitarbeiter *m*	temporary worker
Zeitarbeitsfirma *f*	temp agency *(coll.)* temporary work agency temporary employment agency
Zement *m*	cement
Zementklinker *m*	cement clinker
Zentrierwinkel *m*	center finder *(AE)* centre finder *(BE)*
Zentrumsfinder *m*	center finder *(AE)* centre finder *(BE)*
zerbrechlich	fragile
zerbrochen	broken
Zieh-Schabhobel *m*	pullshave
Ziehklinge *f*	cabinet scraper card scraper
Ziehklingenhobel *m*	scraping plane
Ziehklingenschaber *m*	chair devil
Ziehmesser *n*	drawknife
ziemlich	fairly
Zimmermannsaxt *f*	broad ax *(AE)* broad axe *(BE)*

German	English
Zimmermannsbeil *n*	carpenter's hatchet
Zimmermannsbeitel *m*	firmer chisel
Zimmermannswinkel *m*	framing square
Zink *nsg*	zinc *sg*
Zinkensäge *f*	dovetail saw
Zinkenschablone *f*	dovetail marker
	dovetail saddle marker
Zinkenschmiege *f*	dovetail bevel
Zinkenstemmeisen *n*	dovetail chisel
Zinkenwinkel *m*	dovetail square
Zinn *nsg*	tin *sg*
Zollstock *m*	folding rule
zufrieden sein mit	content with, to be
Zugmesser *n*	drawknife
Zugsäge *f*	pit saw
Zungenkelle *f*	tongue trowel
zur Verfügung stellen	available, to make
Zusammenarbeit *f*	collaboration
	cooperation
Zustand *m*	condition
zuständig sein für etwas	charge of something, to be in
zuverlässig	reliable
zuvorkommend	obliging
Zwinge *f*	clamp
Zwölfeck *n*	dodecagon
zylindrisch	cylindrical

Z

English – German

A

accident	Unfall *m*
accident at work	Arbeitsunfall *m*
accident prevention regulations *pl*	Unfallverhütungsvorschriften/ UVV *fpl*
acetone *sg*	Aceton *nsg* Azeton *nsg*
Achilles' heel *(coll.)*	Achillesferse *f (ugs.)*
acid	Säure *f*
acid density	Säuredichte *f*
acid-free	säurefrei
acid-proof	säurebeständig säureresistent
acid-resistant	säurebeständig säureresistent
acryl paint	Acrylfarbe *f*
acrylic *sg*	Acryl *nsg*
address	Adresse *f* Anschrift *f*
adhesive tape	Klebeband *n*
adjustable bow	verschiebbarer Bügel *m*
adjustable spanner *(BE)*	Engländer *m* Rollgabelschlüssel *m*
adjustable wrench *(BE)*	Engländer *m* Rollgabelschlüssel *m*
advice	Avis *m/n*
advise, to	beraten
adz *(AE)*	Dechsel *f* Dachsbeil *n* Querbeil *n*
adze *(BE)*	Dechsel *f* Dachsbeil *n* Querbeil *n*

aerosol can	Spraydose *f*
	Sprühdose *f*
afternoon	Nachmittag *m*
against all odds	allen Widrigkeiten zum Trotz
	entgegen allen Erwartungen
	gegen alle Schwierigkeiten
air conditioner	Klimaanlage *f*
air conditioning	Klimaanlage *f*
air moisture *sg*	Luftfeuchtigkeit *fsg*
	Luftfeuchte *fsg*
air *sg*	Luft *fsg*
alarm	Alarm *m*
alarm system	Alarmanlage *f*
alcohol	Alkohol *m*
all-steel screw clamp	Ganzstahlzwinge *f*
Allen key	Inbusschlüssel *m* (® Ruia Group)
(® Allen Manufacturing Company)	Innensechskant-Schraubendreher
	m
	Inbus *m* (® Ruia Group)
Allen screw	Innensechskantschraube *f*
(® Allen Manufacturing Company)	
Allen wrench	Inbusschlüssel *m* (® Ruia Group)
(® Allen Manufacturing Company)	Inbus *m* (® Ruia Group)
alloyed steel	legierter Stahl *m*
aluminium *sg (BE)*	Aluminium *nsg*
aluminum *sg (AE)*	Aluminium *nsg*
anchor point	Anschlagpunkt *m*
angle	Winkel *m*
angle gauge	Winkellehre *f*
angle grinder	Flex *f* (® FLEX Elektrowerkzeuge
	GmbH)
	Winkelschleifer *m*
	Trennschleifer *m*

annual	jährlich
anvil	Amboss *m*
April	April *m*
arc	Bogen *m*
Archimedean drill	Drillbohrer *m*
architect	Architekt *m*
argon *sg*	Argon *nsg*
asbestos	Asbest *m*
ash handle	Eschenstiel *m*
attention *sg*	Achtung *fsg*
August	August *m*
autoclaved aerated concrete/AAC	Porenbeton *m* Gasbeton *m*
autoclaved cellular concrete/ACC	Porenbeton *m* Gasbeton *m*
autoclaved lightweight concrete/ALC	Porenbeton *m* Gasbeton *m*
automatic center punch *(AE)*	Automatikkörner *m*
automatic centre punch *(BE)*	Automatikkörner *m*
automatic darkening filter/ADF	automatischer Schweißerschutzfilter *m*
available, to make	bereitstellen zur Verfügung stellen
avoid, to	vermeiden
awl	Ahle *f*
ax *(AE)*	Axt *f*
ax handle *(AE)*	Axtstiel *m*
axe *(BE)*	Axt *f*
axe handle *(BE)*	Axtstiel *m*

B

B

back	hinten
back saw	Rücksäge *f*
back, at the	hinten
backward *(AE)*	rückwärts
backwards *(BE)*	rückwärts
bad	schlecht
ball peen hammer *(AE)*	Kugelhammer *m*
ball pein hammer *(BE)*	Kugelhammer *m*
ban on alcohol	Alkoholverbot *n*
bank holiday *(BE)*	Bankfeiertag *m*
banksman	Einweiser *m* (z.B. Kran, LKW)
bark spud	Schäleisen *n*
barrel	Fass *n*
	Tonne *f*
barrel draw knife	Fassschaber *m*
barrette file	Barettfeile *f*
bastard (coarse)	Hieb 1 *m*
	bastard (grob)
bead forming tool	Rundprofileisen *n*
beam compass heads *pl*	Stangenzirkelspitzen *fpl*
beautiful	schön
beeswax	Bienenwachs *n*
Belgian whetstone	Belgischer Brocken *m*
bell	Klingel *f*
	Türklingel *f*
belt sander	Bandschleifer *m*
bench plane	Flächenhobel *m*
bent	gebogen
besom	Reisigbesen *m*
beveled steel square *(AE)*	Haarwinkel *m*

bevelled steel square *(BE)*	Haarwinkel *m*
bib overalls *pl (AE)*	Latzhose *f*
big (volume/mass)	groß
bilge pump	Lenzpumpe *f*
bitumen	Bitumen *n*
blacksmith's hammer	Schmiedehammer *m*
blade	Klinge *f*
blade adjustment hammer	Hammer zum Justieren von Hobeleisen *m*
blank flange	Blindflansch *m*
blast furnace slag cement	Hochofenzement *m*
blind flange	Blindflansch *m*
block plane	Blockhobel *m* Einhandhobel *m*
blue-collar worker *(coll.)*	Arbeiter *m*
blumb bob	Senklot *n*
body	Korpus *m*
body clamp	Korpuszwinge *f*
boiled linseed oil	Leinölfirnis *m*
bolt cropper	Bolzenschneider *m*
bolt cutter	Bolzenschneider *m*
bordering hammer	Sickenhammer *m*
boring	langweilig
borrow, to	borgen
bottom	untere unterer unteres
bottom cleaning chisel	Grundeisen *n*
bottom valve	Bodenventil *n*
bottom, at the	unten
bow saw	1. Bogensäge *f* 2. Schittersäge *f*

B

bow saw blade	Schittersägeblatt n
bowl finishing tool	Schalenschlichtstahl m
bowl gouge	Schalenröhre f
bowl maker's adze (BE)	Hohldechsel m
box cutter	Teppichmesser n Cuttermesser n
brass	Messing n
brass brush	Messingbürste f
brass hammer	Messinghammer m
brass-head mallet	Klüpfel mit Messingkopf m
brick	Mauerstein m
brick cutting chisel	Fugenmeißel m
brick mason's hammer	Maurerhammer m
bricklayer's chisel	Maurermeißel m
bricklayer's hammer	Maurerhammer m
broad ax (AE)	Zimmermannsaxt f
broad axe (BE)	Zimmermannsaxt f
broad brush	Quast m
broken	zerbrochen
bronze-head mallet	Klüpfel mit Bronzekopf m
broom	Besen m
brush	1. Bürste f 2. Pinsel m
brush cleaner	Pinselreiniger m
bucket	Eimer m
built on sand, to be (coll.)	auf tönernen Füßen stehen (ugs.)
bung wrench	Fassschlüssel m
Bunsen burner	Bunsenbrenner m
burr	Grat m
business day	1. Arbeitstag m 2. Werktag m (in UK/USA keine Unterscheidung)

business premises *pl*	Geschäftsräume *mpl*
busy	beschäftigt
butt chisel	Stummelstechbeitel *m*
	Kurzbeitel *m*
buzz saw *(AE)*	Kreissäge *f*

C

C-clamp	C-Zwinge *f*
cabinet scraper	1. Furnierschabhobel *m*
	2. Ziehklinge *f*
cabinetmaker's hammer	Tischlerhammer *m*
	Schreinerhammer *m*
cabinetmaker's hammer,	Tischlerhammer,
French pattern	französische Form *m*
	Schreinerhammer,
	französische Form *m*
cabinetmaker's mallet	Schreinerklüpfel *m*
	Tischlerklüpfel *m*
cable	Kabel *n*
cable drum	Kabeltrommel *f* (Erdkabel)
cable reel	Kabeltrommel *f*
	(Verlängerungsleitung)
cable shears *pl*	Kabelschere *f*
cable stripping knife	Abisoliermesser *n*
calculate, to	kalkulieren
caliper	Schieblehre *f*
	Messschieber *m*
captive ring tool	Ringschneider *m*
carbon steel	Kohlenstoffstahl *m*
carcass saw *(AE)*	Rückensäge *f*
card scraper	Ziehklinge *f*
cardboard box	Kartonschachtel *f*
	Pappkarton *m (ugs.)*

C

careful	1. sorgfältig 2. vorsichtig
careless	1. unvorsichtig 2. fahrlässig
carpenter's ax *(AE)*	Tischlerbeil *n*
carpenter's axe *(BE)*	Tischlerbeil *n*
carpenter's gauge	Tischlerzirkel *m*
carpenter's hatchet	Zimmermannsbeil *n*
carpenter's mallet	Klopfholz *n*
carpenter's pincers *pl*	Kneifzange *f*
carpenter's roofing hammer	Latthammer *m*
carpet	Teppich *m*
cartridge	Kartätsche *f*
casing	Schalung *f*
cast steel	Gussstahl *m*
caulking gun	Fugenpistole *f*
cause	Ursache *f*
caustic soda *sg*	Ätznatron *nsg*
CE mark	CE-Kennzeichnung *f*
CE marking	CE-Kennzeichnung *f*
cell phone *(AE)*	Mobiltelefon *n* Handy *n*
cell phone number *(AE)*	Mobilnummer *f* Mobiltelefonnummer *f* Handynummer *f*
cellular concrete saw	Porenbetonsäge *f*
cellular phone *(AE)*	Mobiltelefon *n* Handy *n*
Celsius	Celsius *n*
cement	Zement *m*
cement clinker	Zementklinker *m*
cement groover	Dehnungsfugenkelle *f*

cement mixer	Betonmischer *m*
center finder *(AE)*	Zentrierwinkel *m* Zentrumsfinder *m* Mittelpunktfinder *m*
center punch *(AE)*	Körner *m*
centre finder *(BE)*	Zentrierwinkel *m* Zentrumsfinder *m* Mittelpunktfinder *m*
centre punch *(BE)*	Körner *m*
chain	Kette *f*
chair devil	Ziehklingenschaber *m*
chairmaker's scraper	Stuhlmacher-Ziehklingenschaber *m*
chalk	Kreide *f*
chalk line	Schlagschnur *f*
chamfer plane	Fasenhobel *m*
charge of something, to be in	zuständig sein für etwas
charge, to	berechnen (fin.)
checked face	rauhe Bahn *f* (gekerbte Schlagfläche)
chemical	Chemikalie *f*
chipboard	Spanplatte *f*
chipboard screw	Spanplattenschraube *f*
chisel	1. Beitel *m* / Stemmeisen *n* / Stecheisen *n* / Stechbeitel *m* 2. Meißel *m*
chisel edge guard	Schneidenschutz für Stemmeisen *m*
choose, to	auswählen aussuchen
chop saw	Kappsäge *f*
chrome plated	verchromt
chrome *sg*	Chrom *nsg*

C

C

chuck key	Bohrfutterschlüssel *m*
circle	Kreis *m*
circlip pliers for external rings *pl*	Sicherungsringzange für Außenringe *f*
circlip pliers for internal rings *pl*	Sicherungsringzange für Innenringe *f*
circlip pliers *pl*	Sicherungsringzange *f*
circular saw *(BE)*	Kreissäge *f*
circumference (only circle)	Umfang *m* (nur Kreis)
clamp	Zwinge *f*
claw hammer, English pattern	Englischer Klauenhammer *m*
clean	sauber
cleaned	gereinigt
clear coat	Klarlack *m*
clear lacquer	Klarlack *m*
client	1. Kunde *m* 2. Auftraggeber *m*
clinker	Klinker *m*
clock	Uhr *f*
cloudburst	Wolkenbruch *m*
club hammer	Fäustel *m*
coarse stone	Schruppstein *m*
cobbler's hammer	Schusterhammer *m*
cold	kalt
cold cleaner	Kaltreiniger *m*
collaboration	Zusammenarbeit *f*
colleague	Kollege *m* Arbeitskollege *m*
coloured concrete	farbiger Beton *m*
comb pliers *pl*	Kombizange *f*
combi pliers *pl*	Kombizange *f*
combination pliers *pl*	Kombizange *f*

combination square	Kombinationswinkel *m*
combination stone	Kombischleifstein *m*
communication	Kommunikation *f*
company premises *pl*	Betriebsgelände *n*
compass plane	Schiffshobel *m*
complaint	1. Reklamation *f*
	2. Beschwerde *f*
comply with, to	1. entsprechen (z.B. Bedingungen)
	2. einhalten (z.B. Vorschriften)
	3. erfüllen (z.B. Frist)
compressed	verdichtet
compressed air *sg*	Druckluft *fsg*
concrete	Beton *m*
	Normalbeton *m*
concrete drill	Betonbohrer *m*
concrete mixer	Betonmischer *m*
concrete pliers *pl*	Monierzange *f*
	Rabitzzange *f*
	Flechterzange *f*
	Betonzange *f*
concrete spreader	Betonverteiler *m*
	Betonschieber *m*
concretor's pliers *pl*	Monierzange *f*
	Rabitzzange *f*
	Flechterzange *f*
	Betonzange *f*
condition	1. Zustand *m*
	2. Bedingung *f*
conical gouge slip stone	kegelförmiger Bilderhauer-schleifstein *m*
consistent	konsequent
contact details *pl*	Kontaktdaten *pl*
content with, to be	zufrieden sein mit
control square	Kontrollwinkel *m*

C

cooperation	Zusammenarbeit *f*
coping saw	Dekupiersäge *f* Laubsäge *f*
copper hammer	Kupferhammer *m*
copper plated	verkupfert
copper *sg*	Kupfer *nsg*
cord	Maurerschnur *f*
cordless screwdriver	Akkuschrauber *m*
cork	Kork *m*
cork flooring	Korkboden *m*
corner brush	Eckenpinsel *m*
corner clamp	Rahmenspanner *m*
corner cutting chisel	Eckenausstecheisen *n*
corner pipe wrench	Eckrohrzange *f*
correction powder	Korrekturpulver *n*
corroded	korrodiert
corrosive	ätzend
count, to	zählen
countersink	Senker *m*
cover sheeting	Abdeckfolie *f*
crack	Riss *m*
crane driver	Kranführer *m*
crane driver licence *(BE)*	Kranführerschein *m*
crane driver's license *(AE)*	Kranführerschein *m*
crane operator	Kranführer *m*
crane operator licence *(BE)*	Kranführerschein *m*
crane operator's license *(AE)*	Kranführerschein *m*
crane work *sg*	Kranarbeiten *fpl*
cranked paring chisel	Stechbeitel mit geschwungener Klinge *m* Stufenstechbeitel *m*
crescent wrench *(AE)*	Engländer *m* Rollgabelschlüssel *m*

crimping pliers *pl*	Crimpzange *f*
crimping tool	Crimpzange *f*
cross pein hammer *(BE)*	Schlosserhammer *m*
cross pein hammer, English pattern *(BE)*	Schlosserhammer, englische Form *m*
cross pein hammer, German pattern *(BE)*	Schlosserhammer, deutsche Form *m*
cross peen hammer *(AE)*	Schlosserhammer *m*
cross peen hammer, English pattern *(AE)*	Schlosserhammer, englische Form *m*
cross peen hammer, German pattern *(AE)*	Schlosserhammer, deutsche Form *m*
cross-cut	Kreuzhieb *m*
cross-cut blade	Absetzsägeblatt *n*
cross-cut chisel	Kreuzmeißel *m*
cross-cut file	Kreuzhieb-Feile *f*
crosscut	Querschnitt *m*
crosscut saw	Absetzsäge *f*
crossing file	Vogelzungenfeile *f*
crowbar	1. Stemmeisen *n* / Brechstange *f* / Brecheisen *n* 2. Nageleisen *n* / Kuhfuß *m*
crucible tongs *pl*	Bauchzange *f* Tiegelzange *f*
curious	neugierig
cut	Hieb *m*
cut 1 (coarse)	Hieb 1 *m* bastard (grob)
cut 2 (middle)	Hieb 2 *m* halbschlicht (mittel)
cut 3 (fine)	Hieb 3 *m* schlicht (fein)
cylinder rack	Flaschenhalterung *f*
cylindrical	zylindrisch

C

D

daily	täglich
dangerous	gefährlich
date	Datum *n*
day	Tag *m*
day after tomorrow, the *sg*	übermorgen
day before yesterday, the *sg*	vorgestern
December	Dezember *m*
decibel level	Schallpegel *m*
defect description	Fehlerbeschreibung *f*
degree	Grad *m*
delay	1. Verzögerung *f* 2. Verspätung *f*
delay, to	1. aufschieben 2. verzögern 3. verschieben
depth	Tiefe *f*
detail	Einzelheit *f* Detail *n*
diagonal cut	Diagonalschnitt *m*
diagonal cutter	Seitenschneider *m*
diameter	Durchmesser *m*
diamond parting tool	Abstechstahl Diamantform *m*
diamond sharpener	Diamantschleifer *m*
diamond sharpening plate	Diamantschleifplatte *f*
diamond sharpening stone	Diamantschleifstein *m*
die stock	Schneidkluppe *f*
different	anders unterschiedlich
difficult	schwer schwierig
diligent	1. fleißig 2. sorgfältig
dimension	Abmessung *f*

directions *pl*	Wegbeschreibung *f*
	Anfahrtsbeschreibung *f*
dirt *sg*	Schmutz *msg*
	Dreck *msg*
dirt-sensitive	schmutzempfindlich
dirty	schmutzig
	dreckig
disc grinder	Flex *f* (® FLEX Elektrowerkzeuge GmbH)
	Winkelschleifer *m*
	Trennschleifer *m*
discard, to	1. aussondern
	2. ausrangieren
	3. ausscheiden
	4. ablegen
dishonest	unehrlich
dishpan hands *pl (coll.)*	Spülhände *fpl (ugs.)*
do a good job, to	gute Arbeit leisten
dodecagon	Zwölfeck *n*
dolly *(AE)* (tool)	Sackkarre *f*
	Stechkarre *f*
door	Tür *f*
door frame	Türrahmen *m*
door handle	Türdrücker *m*
	Türklinke *f*
door lock	Türschloss *n*
door stop	Türstopper *m*
door stopper	Türstopper *m*
doorbell	Klingel *f*
	Türklingel *f*
double doors *pl*	Doppeltür *f*
double square	Winkel mit verschiebbarem Anschlag *m*
double-cut	Kreuzhieb *m*
double-cut file	Kreuzhieb-Feile *f*

D

double-faced	beidseitig
dovetail bevel	Zinkenschmiege *f*
dovetail chisel	Zinkenstemmeisen *n*
dovetail marker	Zinkenschablone *f*
dovetail plane	Grathobel *m*
dovetail saddle marker	Zinkenschablone *f*
dovetail saw	Schwalbenschwanzsäge *f*
	Zinkensäge *f*
dovetail square	Zinkenwinkel *m*
drain	1. Straßenablauf *m* / Gully *m/n*
	2. Abfluss *m*
drain valve	Entleerungsventil *n*
drawing pin *(BE)*	Reißzwecke *f*
	Heftzwecke *f*
	Reißnagel *m*
drawknife	Zugmesser *n*
	Ziehmesser *n*
drill	Drillbohrer *m*
drill bit	Bohrer *m* (für Bohrmaschine)
drill chuck	Bohrfutter *n*
drizzle	Nieselregen *m*
	Niesel *m*
drum trolley	Fasskarre *f*
dry	trocken
dry wood	trockenes Holz *n*
drywall *(AE)*	1. Rigipsplatte *f* (® Saint-Gobain Rigips GmbH) / Gipskartonplatte/GKP *f* / Gipskarton-Bauplatte/GKB *f*
	2. Gipswandbauplatte *f*
drywall hammer	Gipserhammer *m*
	Gipserbeil *n*
dual marking gauge	Zapfenstreichmaß mit 2 Messerrädern *n*
duck tape	Panzerband *n*

D

duct tape	Panzerband n
dull	stumpf
dungarees pl (BE)	Latzhose f
dust	Staub m
dust-sensitive	staubempfindlich
dustpan	Kehrblech n
	Kehrschaufel f
dusty	staubig

E

ear plug	Ohrstöpsel m
	Ohrenstöpsel m
ear protection	Ohrenschützer fpl Gehörschutz m
easy	leicht (mühelos)
	einfach
eaves pl	Dachtraufe f
	Traufe f
edge trimmer	Kantenhobel m
effective	effektiv
effectiveness	Effektivität fsg
efficiency	Effizienz f
efficient	effizient
electric	elektrisch
electric torch (BE)	Taschenlampe f
electrical tape	Isolierband n
electrician's chisel	Elektrikermeißel m
electrician's splitting chisel	Elektrikerschlitzmeißel m
electronic digital caliper	elektronischer Digital-Mess-schieber m
electronic pliers pl	Elektronikzange f
elevator (AE) (lift)	Aufzug m
	Fahrstuhl m
	Lift m
emulsion paint	Dispersionsfarbe f

engine oil	Motoröl *n*
entrenching tool	Klappspaten *m*
environment	Umwelt *fsg*
especially	1. speziell
	2. besonders
	3. insbesondere
evening	Abend *m*
exact	genau
excellent	ausgezeichnet
exciting	aufregend
	spannend
extension	Verlängerung *f*
extension cord *(AE)*	Verlängerungsschnur *f*
extension lead *(BE)*	Verlängerungsschnur *f*
external Torx screw (® acument)	Außen-Torx-Schraube *f*
	(® acument)
extraordinary	außergewöhnlich

F

factory	Fabrik *f*
factory security office	Werkschutz *msg*
factory security service	Werkschutz *msg*
faded	verblichen
Fahrenheit	Fahrenheit *n*
fair faced concrete	Sichtbeton *m*
fairly	ziemlich
falsework	Lehrgerüst *n*
fast	schnell
fault	Verschulden *nsg*
fax	Fax *m/n*
	Telefax *m/n*
fax number	Faxnummer *f*
	Telefaxnummer *f*

February	Februar *m*
feeler gauge	Fühlerlehre *f*
file	Feile *f*
filling knife	Füllspachtel *f/m*
fillister plane	Falzhobel *m* Simshobel *m*
fine honing stone	Feinstabziehstein *m*
fire blanket	Löschdecke *f* Feuerlöschdecke *f*
fire extinguisher	Feuerlöscher *m*
fire protection sign	Brandschutzzeichen *n*
firmer chisel	Zimmermannsbeitel *m*
firmer gouge	Hohlbeitel *m*
first aid box	Verbandskasten *m*
first aid kit	Verbandskasten *m*
fixed bow	fester Bügel *m*
flammable	entzündlich
flashlight *(AE)*	Taschenlampe *f*
flat adz *(AE)*	Flachdechsel *m*
flat adze *(BE)*	Flachdechsel *m*
flat brush	Flachpinsel *m*
flat chisel	Flachmeißel *m*
flat file	Flachfeile *f*
flat pliers *pl*	Flachzange *f*
flat round pliers *pl*	Flachrundzange *f*
flat-nose pliers *pl*	Flachzange *f*
flattening stone	Abrichtblock *m* (Siliziumkarbid) Schärfsteinabrichtblock *m* (Siliziumkarbid)
flexible	flexibel
float	Reibebrett *n*
floor	1. Boden *m* 2. Etage *f*

F

floor scraper	Stoßscharre *f*
flooring trowel	Bodenlegerkelle *f*
flush cutting saw	flexible Dübelsäge *f*
fly ash	Flugasche *f*
foam	Schaum *m*
folding rule	Gliedermaßstab *m*
	Zollstock *m*
	Meterstab *m*
folding spade	Klappspaten *m*
foreman	1. Vorarbeiter *m*
	2. Polier *m*
forget to do something, to	vergessen etwas zu tun
formaldehyde *sg*	Formaldehyd *msg/nsg*
formwork	Schalung *f*
Forstner bit	Forstnerbohrer *m*
Forstner drill	Forstnerbohrer *m*
fortnight *(BE)*	vierzehn Tage *mpl*
forward *(AE)*	vorwärts
forwards *(BE)*	vorwärts
fragile	zerbrechlich
frame	Rahmen *m*
frame saw	Gestellsäge *f*
	Spannsäge *f*
framing gauge	Blockhaus-Hohlbeitel *m*
framing square	Zimmermannswinkel *m*
fresh concrete	Frischbeton *m*
fret saw	Laubsäge *f*
fret saw table	Laubsägetischchen *n*
fret wire saw	Bundschlitzsäge für Gitarren *f*
fretsaw blade	Laubsägeblatt *n*
Friday	Freitag *m*
friendly	freundlich

F

froe	Schindelspalthacke f
front, at the	vorne
fully synthetic	vollsynthetisch
functional testing	Funktionsprüfung f
funnel	Trichter m

G

G-clamp	C-Zwinge f
gaffer tape	Gafferband n
galvanized	galvanisiert
gas	Gas n
gas (AE)	Benzin n
gas cylinder	Gasflasche f
gas detector	Gasmelder m
gasoline (AE)	Benzin n
gent's saw	Feinsäge f
German Industrial Standard/DIN	Deutsche Industrienorm/DIN f
gimlet	Vorbohrer m
	Nagelbohrer m.
glass cutter	Glasschneider m
glass paper	Glaspapier n
glass wool	Glaswolle f
glossy	glänzend
glue gun	Klebepistole f
	Leimpistole f
goggles pl	Schutzbrille f
good	gut
goose neck	Schwanenhals m
graduation	Skalierung f
grain	Körnung f
granite	Granit m
graphite	Graphit m

G

grateful	dankbar
graupel	Graupel *f*
gravel	Kies *m*
grease gun	Fettpresse *f*
	Schmierpresse *f*
grease, to	einfetten
	schmieren
grind, to	schruppen
grinding stick	Schleifstab *m*
grinding wheel	Schleifscheibe *f*
gripping pliers *pl*	Gripzange *f*
	Feststellzange *f*
	Festklemmzange *f*
groove joint pliers *pl*	Wasserpumpenzange *f*
grooving chisel	Nutenmeißel *m*
guitar saw	Bundschlitzsäge für Gitarren *f*
gun oil	Waffenöl *n*
gypsum	Gips *m*
gypsum board *(AE)*	1. Rigipsplatte *f* (® Saint-Gobain Rigips GmbH) / Gipskarton-platte/GKP *f* / Gipskarton-Bauplatte/GKB *f*
	2. Gipswandbauplatte *f*
gypsum plasterboard	Gipsplatte *f*
gypsum plasterboard *(BE)*	1. Rigipsplatte *f* (® Saint-Gobain Rigips GmbH) / Gipskarton-platte/GKP *f* / Gipskarton-Bauplatte/GKB *f*
	2. Gipswandbauplatte *f*
gypsum wallboard *(AE)*	1. Rigipsplatte *f* (® Saint-Gobain Rigips GmbH) / Gipskartonplatte/GKP *f* / Gipskarton-Bauplatte/GKB *f*
	2. Gipswandbauplatte *f*

G

H

hacksaw	1. Eisensäge *f* 2. Bügelsäge *f*
hail	Hagel *msg*
hairline crack	feiner Riss *m*
half round file	Halbrundfeile *f*
half smooth *sg* (middle)	Hieb 2 *m* halbschlicht (mittel)
half-round (middle)	halbrund (mitte)
hammer	Hammer *m*
hammer drill	Schlagbohrmaschine *f*
hammer handle	Hammerstiel *m*
hammer holder	Hammerbügel *m*
hand brush	Handfeger *m* Handbesen *m*
hand scraper	Schaber *m*
hand screw clamp	Parallel-Schraubzwinge *f*
hand truck *(AE)*	Sackkarre *f* Stechkarre *f*
hand-shovel	Handschaufel *f*
handle	Heft *n*
handsaw	Fuchsschwanz *m*
hard (consistency)	hart (Konsistenz)
hard	schwer schwierig
hard hat	Schutzhelm *m*
hardboard	Hartfaserplatte *f*
hardened	gehärtet
hardwood	Hartholz *n*
hardwood saw	Hartholzsäge *f*
harpoon chisel	Harpuneneisen *n*
hatchet	Beil *n*

hazardous waste	gefährlicher Abfall *m*
	Giftmüll *msg*
	Sondermüll *msg*
	Sonderabfall *m*
heat *sg*	Hitze *fsg*
heavy	schwer (Masse)
heavyweight concrete	Schwerbeton *m*
height	Höhe *f*
help, to	helfen
helpful	hilfsbereit
hemp cord	Hanfschnur *f*
hex key	Inbusschlüssel *m* (® Ruia Group)
	Innensechskant-Schraubendreher *m*
	Inbus *m* (® Ruia Group)
hexagon	Sechseck *n*
hexagon key	Innensechskant-Schraubendreher *m*
hickory handle	Hickorystiel *m*
hidden nail	versteckter Nagel *m*
high-leverage comb pliers *pl*	Kraft-Kombizange *f*
high-leverage combi pliers *pl*	Kraft-Kombizange *f*
high-leverage combination pliers *pl*	Kraft-Kombizange *f*
high-leverage diagonal cutter	Kraftseitenschneider *m*
highly flammable	hochentzündlich
hinge	Scharnier *n*
hoarfrost	Raureif *msg*
hoisting equipment	Hebezeug *n*
hold down kit	Werkstückniederhalter *m*
hole cutter	Lochsäge *f*
hole punch pliers *pl*	Lochzange *f*

H

hole saw	Lochsäge *f*
holiday	Feiertag *m*
holidays *pl (BE)*	Urlaub *m*
hollow adz *(AE)*	Hohldechsel *m*
hollow adze *(BE)*	Hohldechsel *m*
hollow plane	Rundstabhobel *m*
hollow punch	Locheisen *n*
hollowing tool	Aushöhleisen *n*
hone, to	abziehen
honest	ehrlich
honing compound	Abziehpaste *f*
honing guide	Schärfhilfe *f*
	Schleifführung *f*
honing stone	Abziehstein *m*
honing-oil	Abziehöl *n*
hook	Haken *m*
hornbeam	Weißbuche *f*
horsepower/hp	Pferdestärke/PS *f*
hose	Schlauch *m*
hose clamp	Schlauchschelle *f*
	Schlauchbinder *m*
hose clip	Schlauchschelle *f*
	Schlauchbinder *m*
hot	heiß
hot-glue gun	Heißklebepistole *f*
humidity	Luftfeuchtigkeit *fsg*
	Luftfeuchte *fsg*
hydraulic	hydraulisch
hydrochloric acid	Salzsäure *f*

H

I

ice *sg*	Eis *nsg*
impregnation	Imprägnierung *f*
in time	rechtzeitig (nicht auf den Punkt)
in-situ concrete	Ortbeton *m*
incompatible	unverträglich
inconsistent	inkonsequent
indelible pencil	wasserfester Bleistift *m*
	Tintenstift *m*
	Tintenbleistift *m*
industrial gas	technisches Gas *n*
	industrielles Gas *n*
inform, to	informieren
information *sg*	Information *f*
initials *pl*	Initialen *fpl*
inlay saw	Intarsiensäge *f*
inner corner trowel	Inneneckenkelle *f*
inside caliper	Innentaster *m*
installation	Montage *f*
installation work	Montagearbeit *f*
instruction	1. Weisung *f*
	Anleitung *f*
	2. Unterweisung *f*
insulating tape	Isolierband *n*
interesting	interessant
internal Torx screw (® acument)	Innen-Torx-Schraube *f* (® acument)
invisible	unsichtbar
iron	Eisen *n*
iron casting	Eisenguss *m*
iron-head mallet	Klüpfel mit Eisenkopf *m*

J

jack (tool)	Wagenheber *m*
jack plane	Doppelhobel *m*
	Schlichthobel *m*
January	Januar *m*
Japanese spatula	Japanspachtel *f/m*
jaw	Backe *f*
jerry can	Kanister *m*
jeweller's blade	Juweliersägeblatt *n*
jeweller's saw	Juweliersäge *f*
joiner's bench	Hobelbank *f*
joint trowel	Fugenkelle *f*
jointer plane	Rauhbank *f*
	Raubank *f*
jointing chisel	Fugenmeißel *m*
July	Juli *m*
June	Juni *m*

K

key	Schlüssel *m*
key file	Schlüsselfeile *f*
keyhole saw	Bohrsäge *f*
	Stichling *m*
	Stichsäge *f*
keyless drill chuck	Schnellspannbohrfutter *n*
kilowatt/kW	Kilowatt/kW *n*
knee cushion	Kniekissen *n*
knee pad	Knieschoner *m*
knife	Messer *n*
knife file	Messerfeile *f*
knife shaped parting tool	Abstechstahl Messerform *m*

K

L

ladder	Leiter *f*
laminate	Laminat *n*
laminate flooring	Laminatboden *m*
laminating roller	Laminierwalze *f*
lapping plate	Abrichtblock *m* (Stahl)
	Schärfsteinabrichtblock *m* (Stahl)
large (area)	groß
laser	Laser *m*
last month	letzter Monat
last week	letzte Woche
last year	letztes Jahr
latex paint	Latexfarbe *f*
lathe	Drechselbank *f*
	Drehmaschine *f*
lazy	faul
lead hammer	Bleihammer *m*
lead knife	Bleimesser *n*
lead *sg*	Blei *nsg*
leakage	Leckage *f*
leaked out	ausgelaufen (Flüssigkeit)
learn the hard way, to *(coll.)*	Lehrgeld zahlen *(ugs.)*
leather	Leder *n*
leather honing wheel	Lederabziehscheibe *f*
left	linker/ -e/ -es
	links
left, on the	links
lend, to	ausleihen
	ausborgen
length	Länge *f*
level	Wasserwaage *f*

lever clamp	Hebelzwinge f
lift (BE)	Aufzug m
	Fahrstuhl m
	Lift m
lift, to	anheber (Last)
lifting means pl	Anschlagmittel n
light (mass)	leicht (Masse)
lightweight concrete	Leichtbeton m
lignum vitae	Pockholz n
lime	Kalk m
limestone	Kalkstein m
linoleum knife	Linoleummesser n
linoleum sg	Linoleum nsg
liquid	Flüssigkeit f
little	klein
locking pliers pl	Gripzange f
	Feststellzange f
	Festklemmzange f
long boring tool	Tieflochbohrer m
	(Holzbearbeitung)
long-nose pliers pl	Spitzzange f
long-term	langfristig
loud	laut
low-maintenance	wartungsarm
low-noise	geräuscharm
lubrication gun	Fettpresse f
	Schmierpresse f
lug wrench (AE)	Radkreuz n
	Kreuzschlüssel m
	Drehkreuz n
lumber	Bauholz n
lump hammer	Fäustel m
lunch break	Mittagspause f

L

M

machine	Maschine f
machine cover	Maschinenhülle f
machine screw	Maschinenschraube f
machinist's hammer	Schlosserhammer m
machinist's hammer, English pattern	Schlosserhammer, englische Form m
machinist's hammer, German pattern	Schlosserhammer, deutsche Form m
magnet	Magnet m
magnetic saw guide	magnetische Sägeführung f
magnifying glass	Lupe f
mains tester	Phasenprüfer m
maintainability sg	Wartungsfreundlichkeit fsg
maintenance	Wartung f
maintenance work	Wartungsarbeit f
malleable cast iron screw clamp	Temperguss-Schraubzwinge f
mallet	Holzhammer m
mandatory sign	Gebotszeichen n
manometer	Manometer n
manufacturer	Hersteller m
March	März m
mark	Markierung f
mark, to	markieren
marking	Markierung f
marking gauge	Streichmaß n Zapfenstreichmaß n
marking knife	Anreißmesser n
masking tape	Abdeckband n Abklebeband n Malerkrepp m Kreppband n

mason's hammer	Maurerhammer *m*
mason's hammer, Berlin type	Berliner Maurerhammer *m*
mason's hammer, Rhenish type	Rheinischer Maurerhammer *m*
matt	matt
May	Mai *m*
measurement	1. Messung *f*
	2. Messwert *m*
measuring cup	Messbecher *m*
measuring tape	Maßband *n*
	Bandmaß *n*
measuring wedge	Messkeil *m*
mechanic's nippers *pl*	Monierzange *f*
	Rabitzzange *f*
	Flechterzange *f*
	Betonzange *f*
mechanical	mechanisch
medical glove	Einmalhandschuh *m*
medium-density fibreboard/MDF	mitteldichte Holzfaserplatte/MDF *f*
	mitteldichte Faserplatte/MDF *f*
	MDF-Platte *f*
metal drum	Metallfass *n*
metal scraper	Metallschaber *m*
milling machine	Fräse *f*
	Fräsmaschine *f*
mineral	mineralisch
mineral wool	Mineralwolle *f*
mini gent's saw	Mini-Feinsäge *f*
miter *(AE)*	Gehrung *f*
miter box *(AE)*	Gehrungsschneidlade *f*
	Schneidlade *f*
miter marking saddle *(AE)*	Doppel-Gehrungswinkel *m*
miter saddle *(AE)*	Gehrungsschablone *f*

miter saw *(AE)*	Gehrungssäge *f*
miter square *(AE)*	Gehrungswinkel *m* Gehrmaß *n*
mitre *(BE)*	Gehrung *f*
mitre box *(BE)*	Gehrungsschneidlade *f* Schneidlade *f*
mitre marking saddle *(BE)*	Doppel-Gehrungswinkel *m*
mitre saddle *(BE)*	Gehrungsschablone *f*
mitre saw *(BE)*	Gehrungssäge *f*
mitre square *(BE)*	Gehrungswinkel *m* Gehrmaß *n*
mobile phone *(BE)*	Mobiltelefon *n* Handy *n*
mobile phone number *(BE)*	Mobilnummer *f* Mobiltelefonnummer *f* Handynummer *f*
mobile scaffold	Rollgerüst *n*
modest	bescheiden
moisture *sg*	Feuchtigkeit *fsg*
moisture-proof	feuchtigkeitsbeständig feuchtigkeitsresistent
moisture-sensitive	feuchtigkeitsempfindlich
moldy *(AE)*	schimmelig
Monday	Montag *m*
monier pliers *pl*	Monierzange *f* Rabitzzange *f* Flechterzange *f* Betonzange *f*
monitor, to	überwachen
monkey wrench *(AE)*	Engländer *m* Rollgabelschlüssel *m*
month	Monat *m*

month after next, the *sg*	übernächster Monat
month before last, the *sg*	vorletzter Monat
monthly	monatlich
moonlighting	Schwarzarbeit *f*
morning	1. Morgen *m*
	2. Vormittag *m*
morning break	Frühstückspause *f*
mortar	Mörtel *m*
mortar gun	Mörtelspritzmaschine *f*
mortar tub	Mörtelkübel *m*
mortise and tenon	Schlitz und Zapfen
mortise ax *(AE)*	Lochaxt *f*
	Stemmaxt *f*
	Stichaxt *f*
	Stoßaxt *f*
mortise axe *(BE)*	Lochaxt *f*
	Stemmaxt *f*
	Stichaxt *f*
	Stoßaxt *f*
mortise chisel	Lochbeitel *m*
mortise plane	Einlasseckenhobel *m*
mortising ax *(AE)*	Lochaxt *f*
	Stemmaxt *f*
	Stichaxt *f*
	Stoßaxt *f*
mortising axe *(BE)*	Lochaxt *f*
	Stemmaxt *f*
	Stichaxt *f*
	Stoßaxt *f*
mouldy *(BE)*	schimmelig
mounting set	Montagesatz *m*
multipurpose saw	Mehrzwecksäge *f*

N

nagura stone	Nagurastein *m*
nail	Nagel *m*
nail puller	Nageleisen *n*
	Nagelzieher *m*
nail punch	Nagelversenker *m*
	Nagelsenker *m*
	Nageltreiber *m*
naked flame	offene Flamme *f*
naked light	offenes Licht *n*
natural gas	Erdgas *n*
necessary	1. notwendig
	2. erforderlich
needle	Nadel *f*
needle file	Nadelfeile *f*
needle-nose pliers *pl*	Spitzzange *f*
net	Netz *n*
newton meter/Nm *(AE)*	Newtonmeter/Nm *m/n*
newton metre/Nm *(BE)*	Newtonmeter/Nm *m/n*
next month	nächster Monat
next week	nächste Woche
next year	nächstes Jahr
nickel plated	vernickelt
nickel *sg*	Nickel *nsg*
night	Nacht *f*
no hard feelings *pl (coll.)*	nichts für ungut *(ugs.)*
	Schwamm drüber *(ugs.)*
noble gas	Edelgas *n*
non-flammable	nicht brennbar
noon	Mittag *m*
November	November *m*
nut	Mutter *f* (Werkzeug)
nylon hammer	Nylonhammer *m*

O

obliging	zuvorkommend
octagon	Achteck *n*
October	Oktober *m*
odds and ends *pl (coll.)*	Kleinigkeiten *fpl* Krimskrams *msg (ugs.)*
odds with oneself, to be at	mit sich selbst uneins sein
odds with somebody, to be at	mit jemandem uneins sein mit jemandem uneinig sein
odds with something, to be at	mit etwas in Konflikt stehen
odor *(AE)*	Geruch *m*
odor-free *(AE)*	geruchsneutral
odour *(BE)*	Geruch *m*
odour-free *(BE)*	geruchsneutral
office premises *pl*	Geschäftsräume *mpl*
offset	gekröpft
oil	Öl *n*
oil can	Ölkanne *f*
oil stone	Ölstein *m*
old	alt
on the job	bei der Arbeit
on time	pünktlich (auf den Punkt)
one-hand clamp	Einhandzwinge *f*
one-way glove	Einmalhandschuh *m*
oodles of something *pl (coll.)*	Unmenge von etwas *f*
operating instructions *pl*	Betriebsansweisung *f*
orbital sander	Schwingschleifer *m*
Ordinance on Industrial Safety and Health/BetrSichV	Betriebssicherheitsverordnung/ BetrSichV *f*
outer corner trowel	Außeneckenkelle *f*
outside caliper	Außentaster *m*
outside micrometer *(AE)*	Bügelmessschraube *f* Mikrometerschraube *f* Mikrometer *n*

outside micrometre *(BE)*	Bügelmessschraube *f*
	Mikrometerschraube *f*
	Mikrometer *n*
oval	oval
oval shaped brush	Ovalpinsel *m*
oval skew chisel	ovaler Drehstahl *m*
overlook, to	übersehen
overpressure	Überdruck *m*
overpressure valve	Überdruckventil *n*

P

padlock	Vorhängeschloss *n*
pail	Eimer *m*
paint	Farbe *f*
	Anstrichfarbe *f*
paint can	Farbtopf *m*
paint remover	Abbeizer *m*
	Abbeizmittel *n*
paint roller	Farbroller *m*
	Malerrolle *f*
	Malerwalze *f*
paint stripper	Abbeizer *m*
	Abbeizmittel *n*
paint thinner	Farbverdünner *m*
paint tray	Farbwanne *f*
painter's spatula	Malerspachtel *f/m*
pan tile	Dachpfanne *f*
	Dachziegel *m*
panel	Paneele *f*
parallel clamp	Parallel-Schraubzwinge *f*
paring chisel	1. Trennstemmer *m*
	Stechbeitel *m* (leichter)
	2. Schälbeitel *m*

parquet	Parkett *n*
parquet flooring	Parkettboden *m*
parting tool	Abstechstahl *m*
paste table	Tapeziertisch *m*
pasting table	Tapeziertisch *m*
paving hammer	Pflasterhammer *m*
pentagon	Fünfeck *n*
perimeter	Umfang *m*
petrol *(BE)*	Benzin *n*
Phillips screw (® Phillips Screw Company)	Kreuzschlitzschraube *f*
Phillips screwdriver (® Phillips Screw Company)	Kreuzschlitzschraubendreher *m*
phone	Telefon *n*
phone number	Telefonnummer *f*
pick hammer	Spitzhammer *m*
pickax *(AE)*	Spitzhacke *f*
pickaxe *(BE)*	Spitzhacke *f*
picklock	Dietrich *m*
piercing awl	Stechahle *f*
pin *(BE)*	Reißzwecke *f* Heftzwecke *f* Reißnagel *m*
pin punch	Splinttreiber *m* Splintentreiber *m*
pincers *pl*	Kneifzange *f*
pinch-nose pliers *pl*	Spitzzange *f*
pipe clamp	Rohrzwinge *f* Rohrschelle *f*
pipe clip	Rohrschelle *f*
pipe cutter	Rohrschneider *m* Rohrabschneider *m*

P

pipe vice *(BE)*	Rohrschraubstock *m*
pipe vise *(AE)*	Rohrschraubstock *m*
pipe wrench	Rohrzange *f*
	Schwedenzange *f*
pit saw	Zugsäge *f*
plain face	glatte Bahn *f* (glatte Schlagfläche)
plane	Hobel *m*
plank	Bohle *f*
plaster mixing bowl	Gipsbecher *m*
plasterboard	Gipsplatte *f*
plasterboard *(BE)*	1. Rigipsplatte *f* (® Saint-Gobain Rigips GmbH) / Gipskarton-platte/GKP *f* / Gipskarton-Bauplatte/GKB *f*
	2. Gipswandbauplatte *f*
plasterer's plane	Eckenhobel *m*
plasterer's spatula	Stukkateurspachtel *f/m*
	Gipserspachtel *f/m*
plastic	Kunststoff *m*
plastic hammer	Kunststoffhammer *m*
plastic mallet	Kunststoffhammer *m*
plastic measuring tape	Kunststoffmaßband *n*
plastic saw	Kunststoffsäge *f*
pliers *pl*	Zange *f*
pliers wrench	Zangenschlüssel *m*
plough plane *(BE)*	Nuthobel *m*
plow plane *(AE)*	Nuthobel *m*
plumb bob	Senklot *n*
	Senkblei *n*
plumb bob cord	Senklotschnur *f*
plywood	Sperrholz *n*
plywood floor	Sperrholzboden *m*

P

pneumatic	pneumatisch
pocket caliper	Taschenmessschieber *m*
pocket measuring tape	Taschenbandmaß *n*
pocket plane	Taschenhobel *m*
pointed	spitz
pointed chisel	Spitzmeißel *m*
polite	höflich
polygon	Vieleck *n*
poor work	schlechte Arbeit
Portland cement	Portlandzement *m*
Portland cement clinker	Portlandzementklinker *m*
Portland composite cement	Portlandkompositzement *m*
Portland limestone cement	Portlandkalksteinzement *m*
Portland slag cement	Portlandhüttenzement *m*
post	Pfosten *m*
post level	Wasserwaage für Pfosten *f*
powder	Pulver *n*
Pozidriv screw (® Phillips Screw Company)	Pozidrivschraube *f* (® Phillips Screw Company)
Pozidriv screwdriver (® Phillips Screw Company)	Pozidriv-Scw *m* (® Phillips Screw Company)
precast concrete element	Betonfertigteil *n*
precise	genau präzise
precision sliding bevel	Präzisionsschmiege *f*
precision try square	Präzisionswinkel *m*
precision try square with miter *(AE)*	Präzisionswinkel mit Gehrung *m*
precision try square with mitre *(BE)*	Präzisionswinkel mit Gehrung *m*
premises *pl*	1. Geschäftsräume *mpl* 2. Betriebsgelände *n*
pressure	Druck *m*
pressure gauge	Manometer *n*

P

P

pressure-sensitive	druckempfindlich
prestressed concrete	Spannbeton *m*
price	Preis *m*
pricking awl	Vorstecher *m*
priority	Vorrang *m*
	Priorität *f*
probable	wahrscheinlich
	vermutlich
problem	Problem *n*
producer	Hersteller *m*
profile gauge	Konturschablone *f*
	Profillehre *f*
	Profilabtaster *m*
	Profilschablone *f*
prohibition sign	Verbotszeichen *n*
prohibitory sign	Verbotszeichen *n*
project	Projekt *n*
project manager	Projektleiter *m*
protective clothing	Schutzkleidung *f*
protective glove	Schutzhandschuh *m*
protective shoe	Sicherheitsschuh *m*
protractor	Gradmesser *m*
	Winkelmesser *m*
protractor with halfround head	Gradmesser mit halbrunder Grundplatte *m*
protractor with rectangular head	Gradmesser mit rechteckiger Grundplatte *m*
pry bar	1. Stemmeisen *n* / Brechstange *f* / Brecheisen *n*
	2. Nageleisen *n* / Kuhfuß *m*
pullshave	Zieh-Schabhobel *m*
pump	Pumpe *f*
punctually	pünktlich

push drill	Drillbohrer *m*
push pin	Reißzwecke *f*
	Heftzwecke *f*
	Reißnagel *m*
putty	Kitt *m*
putty knife	Kittmesser *n*

Q

quality	Qualität *f*
quiet	leise

R

rabbet plane *(AE)*	Falzhobel *m*
	Simshobel *m*
Rabitz pliers *pl*	Monierzange *f*
	Rabitzzange *f*
	Flechterzange *f*
	Betonzange *f*
radiator	1. Autokühler *m*
	2. Heizkörper *m*
radiator brush	Heizkörperpinsel *m*
radio	Radio *n*
radio pliers *pl*	Radiozange *f*
radius	Radius *m*
rain	Regen *m*
random orbital sander	Exzenterschleifer *m*
rasp	Raspel *f*
rasp cut	Raspelhieb *m*
ratchet spanner *(BE)*	Knarre *f*
	Ratsche *f*
	Steckschlüssel *m*
ratchet wrench *(AE)*	Knarre *f*
	Ratsche *f*
	Steckschlüssel *m*

R

rawhide hammer	Lederhammer *m*
	Rohhauthammer *m*
ready-mixed concrete	Transportbeton *m*
reamer	Reibahle *f*
	Räumahle *f*
	Räumer *m*
reasonable	vernünftig
rebate plane *(BE)*	Falzhobel *m*
	Simshobel *m*
reciprocating saw	Säbelsäge *f*
rectangular	rechteckig
reel	Haspel *f*/*m*
	Weife *f*
reinforced concrete	Stahlbeton *m*
reliable	zuverlässig
rent out, to	vermieten
rent, to	mieten
repair	Reparatur *f*
repair work	Ausbesserungsarbeit *f*
repair, to	reparieren
replacement blade	Ersatzblatt *n*
rescue ladder	Rettungsleiter *f*
respirator mask	Atemschutzmaske *f*
responsible for something, to be	verantwortlich sein für etwas
restroom *(AE)*	Toilette *f*
	WC *n*
reversible handle	umlegbarer Griff *m*
revolutions per minute/rpm *pl*	Umdrehungen pro Minute / 1/min /
	U/min *fpl (ugs.)*
revolving punch pliers *pl*	Revolverlochzange *f*
right	rechter/ -e/ -es
	rechts
right angle	rechter Winkel *m*

R

right, on the	rechts
rigid	starr
ring	Ring *m*
ring brush	Ringpinsel *m*
ring tool	Ringeisen *n*
rip cut blade	Schlitzsägeblatt *n*
rip saw	Schlitzsäge *f*
ripcut	Längsschnitt *m*
rock wool (® Rockwool)	Steinwolle *f* Rockwolle *f* (® Rockwool)
rod	Stange *f*
rolling scaffold	Rollgerüst *n*
roof	Dach *n*
roof panel	Dachverkleidung *f*
roof shingle	Dachschindel *f*
roof tile	Dachpfanne *f* Dachziegel *m*
roofer's hammer	Dachdeckerhammer *m*
roofing hammer	Latthammer *m*
rope	1. Seil *n* 2. Tau *n*
rotary hammer	Bohrhammer *m*
roughing out gouge	Schruppröhre *f*
roughly	1. ungefähr 2. grob 3. geschätzt
round	rund
round diamond sharpener	runder Diamantschleifer *m*
round file	Rundfeile *f*
round nose scraper	runder Schrotstahl *m*
round profile	Rundprofil *n*
round trowel	Rundkelle *f*

R

rounding plane	Hohlkehlhobel *m*
router plane	Grundhobel *m*
rubber boot	Gummistiefel *m*
rubber glove	Gummihandschuh *m*
rubber holder	Gummihalter *m*
rubber mallet	Gummihammer *m*
rude	unhöflich
ruler (tool)	1. Maßstab *m* 2. Lineal *n*
ruler stop	Anschlag *m* (Stahlmaßstab)
rust	Rost *m*
rust eraser	Rostradierer *m*

S

sack	Sack *m*
sack barrow	Sackkarre *f* Stechkarre *f*
sack truck *(BE)*	Sackkarre *f* Stechkarre *f*
saddle square	Anreißschablone *f*
safety glasses *pl*	Schutzbrille *f*
safety shoe	Sicherheitsschuh *m*
safety sign	Sicherheitszeichen *n*
safety valve	Sicherheitsventil *n*
safety vest	Warnweste *f*
salami tactics *pl (coll.)*	Salamitaktik *f (ugs.)*
sand	Sand *m*
sanding block	Schleifklotz *m*
sandpaper	Schleifpapier *n* Schmirgelpapier *n*
sash saw	Schlitzsäge *f*
Saturday	Samstag *m*

saw	Säge *f*
saw blade	Sägeblatt *n*
saw blade holder	Sägeblatthalter *m*
	Sägeangel *f*
	Sägeblattaufnahme *f*
saw file	Sägefeile *f*
saw file for gent's saw	Feinsägefeile *f*
saw guide	Sägeführung *f*
saw handle	Sägegriff *m*
saw set pliers *pl*	Schränkzange *f*
sawbuck	Sägebock *m* (X-Form)
	Schragen *m* (X-Form)
sawhorse	Sägebock *m* (A-Form)
scabbard chisel	Schlitzbeitel *m*
scaffolding	Gerüst *n*
scaling	Skalierung *f*
scalpel	Skalpell *n*
scissors *pl*	Schere *f*
scoopula	Spatel *f/m*
scrap	Schrott *m*
scrap metal	Schrott *m*
scraper	1. Schaber *m*
	2. Malerspachtel *f/m*
scraper burnisher	Gratzieher *m*
scraping plane	Ziehklingenhobel *m*
screed	Estrich *m*
screw	Schraube *f*
screw anchor *(AE)*	Dübel *m*
screw clamp	1. Schraubzwinge *f*
	2. Schraubschelle *f*
screwdriver	Schraubendreher *m*
scriber	Anreißnadel *f*
	Reißnadel *f*

S

scrub plane	Schrupphobel *m*
sealing washer	Dichtungsring *m*
select, to	auswählen
self-adhesive measuring tape	selbstklebendes Maßband *n*
self-compacting concrete/SCC	selbstverdichtender Beton/SVB *m*
semi-synthetic	teilsynthetisch
sensitive	empfindlich
separate, to	trennen
September	September *m*
serious	ernst
sewing awl	Nähahle *f*
sewing machine oil	Nähmaschinenöl *n*
shackle	Schäkel *m*
sharp-edged	scharfkantig
sharpen, to	schärfen
sharpening machine	Schleifmaschine *f*
sharpening paste	Schleifpaste *f*
sharpening stone	Schärfstein *m*
shed	Schuppen *m*
sheet metal	Blech *n*
sheet metal screw	Blechschraube *f*
sheet steel	Stahlblech *n*
sheetrock (® United States Gypsum Company) *(AE)*	1. Rigipsplatte *f* (® Saint-Gobain Rigips GmbH) / Gipskarton-platte/GKP *f* / Gipskarton-Bauplatte/GKB *f* 2. Gipswandbauplatte *f*
shell auger	Tieflochbohrer *m* (Holzbearbeitung)
shellac	Schellack *m*
shoe hammer	Schusterhammer *m*
short-term	kurzfristig

S

shovel	Schaufel *f*
	Schippe *f*
	Schüppe *f*
shower	Dusche *f*
shut-off valve	Absperrventil *n*
sickle chisel	Sicheleisen *n*
side	Seite *f*
side cutter	Seitenschneider *m*
side cutting scraper	Ausdrehstahl *m* (Holzbearbeitung)
side cutting scraper diamond	Ausdrehstahl trapezoid *m* (Holzbearbeitung)
side cutting scraper round	Ausdrehstahl rund *m* (Holzbearbeitung)
side rabbet plane *(AE)*	Seitenfalzhobel *m*
side rebate plane *(BE)*	Seitenfalzhobel *m*
sieve	Sieb *n*
signature	Unterschrift *f*
silicon carbide	Siliziumkarbid *n*
silicon carbide powder	Silikonkarbidpulver *n*
similar	ähnlich
single-cut	Einhieb *m*
single-cut file	Einhieb-Feile *f*
single-faced	einseitig
size	Größe *f*
skew chisel	1. schräg angeschliffener Flachstahl *m*
	2. Schrägbeitel *m*
skip	Absetzmulde *f*
	Mulde *f*
	Muldencontainer *m*
	Schuttmulde *f*
slant level	Neigungsmessgerät *n*
sledgehammer	Vorschlaghammer *m*

S

sleet	Graupel *f*
sliding bevel	Schmiege *f*
sling gear	Anschlagmittel *n*
sling point	Anschlagpunkt *m*
sling, to	anschlagen
slitting file	Schwertfeile *f*
slotted screw	Schlitzschraube *f*
slotted screwdriver	Schlitzschraubendreher *m*
slow	langsam
slush *sg*	Schneematsch *msg*
small	klein
small hours *pl*	frühe Morgenstunden *fpl*
smoke detector	Rauchmelder *m*
smoking	Rauchen *nsg*
smoking ban	Rauchverbot *n*
smooth (fine)	Hieb 3 *m*
	schlicht (fein)
smoothing plane	Putzhobel *m*
smoothing trowel	Glättekelle *f*
snap-off blade	Abbrechklinge *f*
snipe-nose pliers *pl*	Spitzzange *f*
snow grains *pl*	Griesel *msg*
snow *sg*	Schnee *msg*
snowfall	Schneefall *m*
socket	Steckschlüsseleinsatz *m*
	Nuss *f*
	Stecknuss *f*
socket spanner *(BE)*	Knarre *f*
	Ratsche *f*
	Steckschlüssel *m*
socket wrench *(AE)*	Knarre *f*
	Ratsche *f*
	Steckschlüssel *m*

S

soft (consistency)	weich (Konsistenz)
softwood	Weichholz *n*
solar cell	Solarzelle *f*
solar radiation	Sonneneinstrahlung *f*
soldering iron	Lötkolben *m*
solid rubber tire *(AE)*	Vollgummireifen *m*
solid rubber tyre *(BE)*	Vollgummireifen *m*
solvent	Lösungsmittel *n*
sound level	Schallpegel *m*
spackle knife	Malerspachtel *f/m*
spade	Spaten *m*
spanner *(BE)*	Schraubenschlüssel *m*
spare part	Ersatzteil *n*
Spax screw (® Altenloh, Brinck & Co GmbH & Co. KG)	Spaxschraube *f* (® Altenloh, Brinck & Co GmbH & Co. KG)
specially	1. besonders 2. speziell
specified	1. angegeben 2. festgelegt
spike roller	Stachelroller *m*
spill plane	Fidibushobel *m* Kienspanhobel *m*
spindle gouge	Drehröhre *f*
spindle gouge, English pattern	Drehröhre, englische Form *f*
spindle gouge, European continental pattern	Drehröhre, kontinentale Form *f*
spirit level	Wasserwaage *f*
spirit level unit	Wasserwaagenaufsatz *m*
split, to	aufteilen
splitting chisel	Schlitzmeißel *m*
spokeshave	Schabhobel *m* Schweifhobel *m* Schinder *m*

S

sponge	Schwamm *m*
sponge float	Schwammbrett *n*
spray bottle	Sprühflasche *f*
spray-tight	spritzwasserdicht
spring clamp	Federzwinge *f*
spring steel	Federstahl *m*
spring type divider	Spitzzirkel *m*
square	Winkel *m* (Werkzeug)
	Vierkant *m/n*
square end scraper	gerader Schlichtstahl *m*
	Schaber *m*
	Drechselschaber *m*
square file	Vierkantfeile *f*
square with miter *(AE)*	Winkel mit Gehrung *m*
square with mitre *(BE)*	Winkel mit Gehrung *m*
squared timber	Kantholz *n*
stabbing awl	Anreißnadel *f*
	Ahle *f*
	Reißnadel *f*
stability	Standsicherheit *fsg*
stack, to	stapeln
stainless	rostfrei
stainless steel	Edelstahl *m*
stair saw	Gratsäge *f*
stairmaker's chisel	Treppenbauerbeitel *m*
stairs *pl*	Treppe *f*
stairway	Treppe *f*
standard	Norm *f*
steadiness	Standsicherheit *fsg*
steel	Stahl *m*
steel fibre reinforced concrete	Stahlfaserbeton *m*

S

steel measuring tape	Stahlmaßband *n*
steel rule	Stahlmaßstab *m*
steel square	Stahl-Anschlagwinkel *m*
steel wool *sg*	Stahlwolle *fsg*
stipulated	vereinbart
stone grader	Stein-Präparierer *m*
stork beak pliers *pl*	Storchschnabelzange *f*
storm	Sturm *m*
storm drain	Straßenablauf *m*
	Gully *m/n*
storm sewer *(AE)*	Straßenablauf *m*
	Gully *m/n*
straight	gerade
straight edge	1. Richtscheit *m*
	2. Flachlineal *n*
	3. Haarlineal *n*
strange	merkwürdig
	seltsam
	eigenartig
street broom	Straßenbesen *m*
string line	Maurerschnur *f*
Styrofoam *sg* (® Dow Chemical Company)	Styropor *nsg* (® BASF)
substance	Substanz *f*
sun	Sonne *f*
Sunday	Sonntag *m*
Sunday work	Sonntagsarbeit *f*
supplier	Lieferant *m*
surprised	überrascht
swan neck	Schwanenhals *m*
swan neck chisel	Schwanenhals-Lochbeitel *m*
swan neck shape	gekröpft

S

T

tack *(AE)*	Reißzwecke *f* Heftzwecke *f* Reißnagel *m*
tall (height)	groß
tape gun	Packbandabroller *m*
tape measure	Maßband *n* Bandmaß *n*
tapping screw	Blechschraube *f*
tarpaulin	Plane *f*
technical gas	technisches Gas *n* industrielles Gas *n*
telephone	Telefon *n*
telephone number	Telefonnummer *f*
telephone pliers *pl*	Telefonzange *f*
temp agency *(coll.)*	Zeitarbeitsfirma *f*
temperature	Temperatur *f*
temporary employment	Zeitarbeit *f*
temporary employment agency	Zeitarbeitsfirma *f*
temporary work	Zeitarbeit *f*
temporary work agency	Zeitarbeitsfirma *f*
temporary worker	Zeitarbeiter *m*
tenon saw	Zapfensäge *f*
thick	dick (Gegenstand)
thickness caliper	Dickenmessgerät *n*
thin	dünn (Gegenstand)
thinner	Verdünner *m* Verdünnungsmittel *n*
this month	diesen Monat
this week	diese Woche
this year	dieses Jahr
thousand	tausend

T

thread	Gewinde *n*
thread chaser	Gewindestrehler *m*
threaded rod	Gewindestange *f*
three days ago	vorvorgestern
three-square	Dreikant *m/n*
three-square file	Dreikantfeile *f*
through-crack	durchgehender Riss *m*
thumbtack *(AE)*	Reißzwecke *f*
	Heftzwecke *f*
	Reißnagel *m*
Thursday	Donnerstag *m*
tight	fest
	stramm
tile	Fliese *f*
tile adhesive	Fliesenkleber *m*
tile breaking pliers *pl*	Fliesenbrechzange *f*
tile chisel	Fliesenmeißel *m*
tile cutting and breaking pliers *pl*	Fliesenschneid- und Brechzange *f*
tile cutting machine	Fliesenschneidemaschine *f*
tile hammer	Fliesenhammer *m*
tile hole cutter	Fliesenlochschneider *m*
tile sponge	Fliesenschwamm *m*
tile wedge	Fliesenkeil *m*
tiler's trowel	Fliesenlegerkelle *f*
tilt a window, to	Fenster kippen
tilt valve	Kippventil *n*
timber frame chisel	Blockhausbeitel *m*
tin *sg*	Zinn *nsg*
tin snips *pl*	Blechschere *f*
tin solder *sg*	Lötzinn *nsg*
tincture	Tinktur *f*

T

tire pressure gauge *(AE)*	Reifenluftdruckmesser *m*
tire tread depth gauge *(AE)*	Profiltiefenmesser *m*
tired	müde
today	heute
toilet *(BE)*	Toilette *f*
	WC *n*
tomorrow	morgen
tongue and groove pliers *pl*	Wasserpumpenzange *f*
tongue trowel	Zungenkelle *f*
tool belt	Werkzeuggürtel *m*
tool case	Werkzeugkoffer *m*
tool chest	Werkzeugschrank *m*
tool roll	Rolltasche *f*
toolbox	Werkzeugkasten *m*
toolmaker's hammer	Hammer für Werkzeugmacher *m*
toothed plane	Zahnhobel *m*
top	oberste
	oberster
	oberstes
top, on the	oben
torque	Drehmoment *n*
torque spanner *(BE)*	Drehmomentschlüssel *m*
torque wrench *(AE)*	Drehmomentschlüssel *m*
Torx screw (® acument)	Torxschraube *f* (® acument)
Torx screwdriver (® acument)	Torxschraubendreher *m* (® acument)
trapezoid blade	Trapezklinge *f*
triangular file	Dreikantfeile *f*
tropical wood	Tropenholz *n*
trowel	Maurerkelle *f*
	Kelle *f*
try square	Tischlerwinkel *m*

T

try square with additional function for parallel marking	Tischlerwinkel mit Anreiß-funktion *m*
Tuesday	Dienstag *m*
turning bow saw	Schweifsäge *f*
turning saw blade	Schweifsägeblatt *n*
turpentine	Terpentin *m/n*
tweezers *pl*	Pinzette *f*
type	1. Typ *m* 2. Art *f*
tyre pressure gauge *(BE)*	Reifenluftdruckmesser *m*
tyre tread depth gauge *(BE)*	Profiltiefenmesser *m*

U

ugly	hässlich
ultra high strength concrete/UHSC	ultrahochfester Beton/UHFB *m*
unalloyed steel	unlegierter Stahl *m*
uncleaned	ungereinigt
underfloor heating	Fußbodenheizung *f*
unfriendly	unfreundlich
ungrateful	undankbar
uninteresting	uninteressant
universal saw	Universalsäge *f*
unnecessary	1. unnötig 2. nicht erforderlich
unreasonable	unvernünftig
unreliable	unzuverlässig
urgent	dringend
used oil (e.g. drained from the engine of a vehicle)	Altöl *n*
user guide	Bedienungsanleitung *f* Gebrauchsanleitung *f*
user manual	Bedienungsanleitung *f* Gebrauchsanleitung *f*

U

V

vacation *(AE)*	Urlaub *m*
vacuum	1. Unterdruck *m*
	2. Vakum *n*
vacuum gauge	Vakuummeter *n*
vacuum valve	Unterdruckventil *n*
valve	Ventil *n*
vapor *(AE)*	Dampf *m*
vapor pressure *(AE)*	Dampfdruck *m*
vapour *(BE)*	Dampf *m*
vapour pressure *(BE)*	Dampfdruck *m*
vario corner	Vario-Ecke *f*
varnish	1. Firnis *m*
	2. Lack *m*
vendor	1. Lieferant *m*
	2. Verkäufer *m*
veneer	Furnier *n*
veneer cutter	Furnierschneider *m*
veneer hammer	Furnierhammer *m*
veneer saw	Furniersäge *f*
Venetian blind	Jalousie *f*
vial	Libelle *f*
vibratory plate	Rüttelplatte *f*
vice *(BE)*	Schraubstock *m*
vise *(AE)*	Schraubstock *m*
visual inspection	Sichtprüfung *f*

V

W

wall	Wand *f*
wall plug *(BE)*	Dübel *m*
wallboard *(AE)*	1. Rigipsplatte *f* (® Saint-Gobain Rigips GmbH) / Gipskarton-platte/GKP *f* / Gipskarton-Bauplatte/GKB *f* 2. Gipswandbauplatte *f*
wallpaper	Tapete *f*
wallpaper brush	Tapezierbürste *f*
wallpaper table	Tapeziertisch *m*
warding file	Schlüsselfeile *f*
warm	warm
Warrington hammer (English pattern cabinetmaker's hammer)	Warrington Hammer *m* (Englischer Tischlerhammer)
washer	Unterlegscheibe *f*
water	Wasser *n*
water pump pliers *pl*	Wasserpumpenzange *f*
water vapor *(AE)*	Wasserdampf *m*
water vapour *(BE)*	Wasserdampf *m*
waterstone	Wasserstein *m*
wax	Wachs *n*
weak spot *(coll.)*	Achillesferse *f (ugs.)*
weather	Wetter *n*
weather forecast	Wettervorhersage *f*
Wednesday	Mittwoch *m*
week	Woche *f*
week after next, the *sg*	übernächste Woche
week before last, the *sg*	vorletzte Woche
weekend	Wochenende *n*
weekly	wöchentlich
weight	Gewicht *n*

W

weld seam	Schweißnaht *f*
weld spot	Schweißpunkt *m*
weld-spot, to	punktschweißen
weld, to	schweißen
welder	Schweißer *m*
welders gaiter	Schweißergamasche *f*
welding apron	Schweißerschürze *f*
welding glove	Schweißerhandschuh *m*
welding goggles *pl*	Schweißerbrille *f*
welding grip pliers *pl*	Schweißerzange *f*
welding helmet	Schweißhelm *m*
welding loss	Schweißabbrand *m*
welding machine	Schweißmaschine *f*
welding result	Schweißergebnis *n*
Well done!	Gut gemacht!
Wellington boot	Gummistiefel *m*
wet	nass
wet grinding wheel	Nassschleifmaschine *f*
wheel brace *(BE)*	Radkreuz *n*
	Kreuzschlüssel *m*
	Drehkreuz *n*
wheel loader	Radlader *m*
wheel wrench *(BE)*	Radkreuz *n*
	Kreuzschlüssel *m*
	Drehkreuz *n*
wheelbarrow	Schubkarre *f*
wheeled loader	Radlader *m*
whetstone holder	Schärfsteinhalter *m*
white beech	Weißbuche *f*
white spirit	Terpentinersatz *msg*
	Waschbenzin *n*
white-collar worker *(coll.)*	Angestellter *m*

W

wide	breit
width	Breite *f*
wind	Wind *m*
window	Fenster *n*
window frame	Fensterrahmen *m*
window putty	Fensterkitt *m*
wing screw	Flügelschraube *f*
wire	Draht *m*
wire brush	Drahtbürste *f*
wire stripper	Abisolierzange *f*
wire wool *sg*	Stahlwolle *fsg*
wood bit	Holzbohrer *m* (Einsatz)
wood glue	Holzleim *m*
wood joiner's mallet	Schreinerklüpfel *m*
wood preservative	Holzschutzmittel *n*
wood screw	Holzschraube *f*
wood shavings *pl*	Holzspäne *mpl*
	Hobelspäne *mpl*
	Sägespäne *mpl*
wood stain	Beize *f*
wood treatment	Holzbehandlung *f*
wooden dowel	Holzdübel *m*
wooden wedge	Holzkeil *m*
work accident	Arbeitsunfall *m*
work light	Arbeitsscheinwerfer *m*
work platform	Arbeitsbühne *f*
workbench	Werkbank *f*
working day	1. Arbeitstag *m*
	2. Werktag *m*
	(in UK/USA keine Unterscheidung)
working time	Arbeitszeit *f*
workplace	Arbeitsstätte *f*

W

Workplaces Ordinance/ArbStättV	Arbeitsstättenverordnung/ ArbStättV *f*
wrecking bar	1. Stemmeisen *n* / Brechstange *f* / Brecheisen *n* 2. Nageleisen *n* / Kuhfuß *m*
wrench *(AE)*	Schraubenschlüssel *m*

Y

year	Jahr *n*
year after next, the *sg*	übernächstes Jahr
year before last, the *sg*	vorletztes Jahr
year of construction	Baujahr *n*
year of manufacture	Herstellungsjahr *n*
yesterday	gestern
young	jung

Z

zinc *sg*	Zink *nsg*

Z

Your personal 100 words of everyday life
(general terms)

Your personal 100 words from professional practice
(technical terms)

Your most important notes

Another Technical Dictionary from me!

R I E D E L
Technical Dictionary
Road transport
& more

German – English
English – German

Picture credits